Rose Petal Jam

...
...szy ...oliva ... 6 dkg cukru
...ej ... mieszać na og...
...bo nie zgęstnieje zag...
...rowie n... Gdy zgęstnieje
...o tym ... potem wlać ...
...dkg utartego masła ...
3 żółtki i probukrować
...art przechow...
...mąki 17 dkg masła
...tha wyrobić ciasto ...

Rose Petal Jam

Recipes & Stories
from a Summer in Poland

Beata Zatorska & Simon Target

TABULA BOOKS

Contents

Rose Petal Jam

It was my job, aged five, to gather rose petals to make jam. Each day, together with the local bees, I carefully inspected the deep green, wild rose bushes around the house to search for any newly opened buds. I had to be patient and wait for the June sun to assert itself, and the mountain winds to stop howling at the fragile, early summer days. Finally, one magic morning, a bush would wake up from its green sleep and large pink flowers would greet the rising sun.

The silky soft petals, sparkling with dew, came away easily in my hand, and landed gently on the bottom of my wicker basket. Their rosy fragrance lingered on my fingers for the rest of the day – a true perfume of summer.

My grandmother Józefa simply put the petals in a large stone mortar, covered them with lots of sugar, and blended them into a thick, magenta-coloured paste. She gave me a teaspoonful to savour while she carefully placed every last speck into one of her ready jars. Rose petal jam was her most precious preserve – a dollop of summer to be released in the long winter months when the rose bushes hid under a quilt of snow.

ABOVE Beata, aged two,
helping her grandmother
Józefa in the kitchen.

My Grandmother Józefa's Rose Petal Jam

This fragrant jam is my favourite filling for Polish doughnuts (*pączki*, see page 306). It is best made with fresh petals from the wild rose – *Rosa canina*.

3 OR 4 LARGE HANDFULS FRESH ROSE PETALS

½ KG (ROUGHLY 1 LB) GRANULATED SUGAR

Gather the wild rose petals in the morning, before they have been in the sun too long and released their fragrance.

Place them in a stone mortar or *makutra*. Slowly pour in the sugar and use the pestle to crush the petals together with the sugar. The juice in the petals will gradually blend with the sugar into a deep red, thick paste. No further cooking is needed. The jam can be preserved in sterilized glass jars for up to two years.

A Polish Childhood

I spent the first summers of my life in a tiny village in Lower Silesia in rural Poland. Our house was surrounded by fields of wildflowers so tall a small girl like me could easily disappear from sight. My mother was studying in Kraków, my father doing his compulsory military service, so I was looked after, much of the time, by someone who was to become a big influence on me. Józefa was my grandmother, but I called her "my second mum", Mama Druga.

Józefa worked as a professional chef, but she also cooked for our family, often using many fresh ingredients from her garden. The house was always full of the sweet aromas of food. Nettles and mint hung drying in the attic alongside bunches of chamomile flowers and poppy-seed husks. Yeasty doughnuts (*pączki*) were laid out on every flat surface, stool, and armchair, slowly puffing up under starched white tea towels. Though I was almost too small to hold a rolling pin, Józefa let me roll out the pastry dough to make *pierogi* – the ravioli-like pasta that Poles are addicted to – and taught me cooking secrets told her by her grandmother.

When I was as young as four Mama Druga took me on long walks up into the foothills of the Karkonosze Mountains. I followed close behind, watching the bright flowers on her full skirt dance in front of my eyes.

TOP LEFT "Little Gioconda – Angelina" by Tadeusz Makowski, 1920, from the collection of the National Gallery in Kraków. CENTRE RIGHT Beata, aged three, playing outside in summer.

14

Rose Petal Jam

She stopped half way up the hill to check I was still close by, promising the best view of the village if I kept up. Together we collected herbs and flowers, and she found plants in the woods to make her own medicines and face creams. She taught me the name and use of each one, in cooking and in healing, and did not laugh when I announced my own childish ambition to be a doctor. I only have to close my eyes to remember the smell of her peppermint stomach syrup, her valerian heart drops, and her stinging-nettle arthritis unguent – a potent mix of herbs and compassion that made everyone feel instantly better. A grandma in her 40s, it was as if she was a white witch with shoulder-length chestnut hair and I was her proud apprentice, confident that every illness was curable with her herbs, barks, and ointments.

Every inch of our garden was cultivated with all sorts of vegetables and fruit. Carrots, celeriac, and beetroot would fight for ground space, while dill, peas, and beans knit a tight canopy above them. Calico sacks full of home-grown potatoes, beetroot, and apples were lined in rows on the concrete floor of the cellar, forming secret corridors for me to explore. Throughout the summer Józefa and I would hunt for wild strawberries, blackberries, and raspberries in the mountain forests. We tried not to eat too much fruit while picking and save at least some for our preserves.

Upstairs in the kitchen, recycled glass jars of odd shapes and sizes would clink together in huge tubs of boiling water, ready to be filled with the garden's spoils. The steam glistened in the afternoon sun, casting a silvery web over the windows, the white porcelain cups on the oak dresser, and the large yellow radio in the corner. As the cloud floated higher it condensed on the brass crucifix above the door, and Jesus shed tears rhythmically onto the wooden floor below.

Today when I turn a yellowed page filled with my grandmother's neatly written recipes it is as if I am touching her hand, covered with flour and speckled with diamonds of sugar. I can hear the floorboards creaking under Józefa's feet as she moves between the table and wood-fired stove; I shiver at the sound of a sharp knife scraping the dough from her fingers; I can smell the sweet perfume of her rose petal jam. These memories still run through my head, like the mountain stream through her garden. They are so vivid I can almost fool myself that she is still alive, working as usual at her large oak table, getting her preserves ready for next winter.

TOP RIGHT Józefa's handwritten recipe for *pierogi*. RIGHT Józefa, Beata's grandmother, holding her two-year-old granddaughter in her arms.

17

Rose Petal Jam

Strawberry Fruit Drink § KOMPOT TRUSKAWKOWY

This *kompot* is a summer fruit drink, thinner than the stewed fruit dessert of the same name. It is a refreshing alternative to fizzy drinks for kids, or to beer or wine for adults who prefer not to drink alcohol at lunch and end up sleeping away a warm afternoon. *Kompot* can be made by simply boiling different fruits – apples, pears, blackcurrants – with water, sugar, and spices.

This recipe preserves strawberry *kompot*; my grandmother made it in June, when the strawberries were in season, so we could still enjoy them in chilly December.

ENOUGH FOR 6

1 kg (2 lb 3 oz) FRESH STRAWBERRIES

200 g (7 oz) CASTER (SUPERFINE) SUGAR

1.5 l (3 pints) WATER

Wash the fruit carefully, remove the strawberry stalks (or fruit cores), and place the fresh fruit in 1-litre (2-pint) sterilised jars.

Stir the sugar into the water and bring to the boil. Pour the hot sugar water over the fruit, filling the jars to just below their rims. Stir gently to keep the fruit whole. Screw the lids on firmly.

Place a tea towel or large clean dishcloth in the bottom of a big saucepan and stand the filled jars on it. The towel stops the jars rattling together and breaking when the water in the pan boils. Fill the pan with water to about halfway up the glass jars and bring to the boil with the lid on. The steam created in the pot expands the jar lids.

After 5 minutes, remove the jars from the pan and immediately tighten the lids further before allowing them to cool.

Rose Petal Jam

Józefa took care of the farmhouse and the cooking, while her mother, my great-grandmother Julia, looked after the cellar, the garden, and our ten precious chickens. Nothing was thrown away; even the stinging nettles that constantly invaded the garden through the gaps in the fence would be cut up and dried for chicken feed. Julia wedged her gumboots in the mud as she pulled at the nettles with bare hands, cursing the weed in Russian (saving Polish for her prayers).

In the attic, Julia hung poppies out to dry. Only she knew how to crack open the dried husks to extract the seeds, which Józefa then made into poppy-seed cake (*makowiec*). Down stone steps in the cellar, hundreds of jars of preserved fruits and vegetables were stockpiled for winter. Like precious jewels found at the back of a dark cave, the jars would glow in the light of my torch: golden pear *kompot* – ruby beetroot soup – emerald dill cucumbers – amethyst prune paste. Three women and a cat, we felt secure in this house, safe from winter's bad temper, global depressions, and fumbling regimes.

Pickled Cucumbers OGÓRKI KISZONE

Pickled cucumbers are Poland's most popular side dish, served with meats, cheeses, even made into soup. Drinking the juice from the jar is said to be the best hangover cure known to man (or woman).

1 kg (2 lb 3 oz) SMALL CUCUMBERS

2 l (4 pints) WATER

1 BUNCH DILL

FRUIT TREE LEAVES, e.g. SOUR CHERRY, BLACKCURRANT, OR GRAPE VINE LEAVES (OPTIONAL)

2 CLOVES GARLIC

1 SMALL HORSERADISH ROOT

3 TABLESPOONS SALT

Wash the cucumbers carefully. Don't cut off the ends or pierce the skin in any way. You want the skin to remain crisp while the inside becomes soft. Place the cucumbers in a large glass jar with a sealable lid (4-litre or 8-pint capacity, or you could use 2 x 2-litre jars). The cucumbers fit best if you stand them on end.

Strip the dill leaves from their stems and add to the jar with the whole washed horseradish root and the garlic cloves. On top of all this, place the fruit leaves. These add flavour and with the horseradish help keep the cucumber skins crisp.

Boil the water then add the salt, stirring until it is fully dissolved. When cooled, pour the brine over the cucumbers and herbs so they are completely covered. Seal the lid tightly, making sure the rim is dry to ensure proper suction.

Store in a cool place and leave for 2-3 days before eating.

Rose Petal Jam

Poppy-seed cake § MAKOWIEC

Thanks to a constant supply of poppy seeds from my great-grandmother Julia, we ate poppy-seed cake year round, not just at Christmas. I felt I had a privileged childhood to be offered this sweet, nutty-flavoured cake more often than other children in the village.

MAKES 1 LARGE OR 2 SMALL CAKES

FOR THE POPPY-SEED FILLING

500 g (1 lb 2 oz) POPPY SEEDS

250 ml (8 fl oz) MILK

50 g (2 oz) BUTTER

250 g (9 oz) VANILLA SUGAR

110 g (4 oz) CHOPPED ALMONDS

110 g (4 oz) CHOPPED WALNUTS

ZEST OF ½ LEMON

ALMOND ESSENCE

2 EGG WHITES

FOR THE CAKE

110 g (4 oz) BUTTER

150 g (5 oz) CASTER (SUPERFINE) SUGAR

2 EGG YOLKS

250 ml (8 fl oz) FULL CREAM MILK

500 g (1 lb 2 oz) PLAIN (ALL-PURPOSE) FLOUR

40 g (1 ½ oz) DRIED YEAST

100 g (3 ½ oz) SULTANAS OR GOLDEN RAISINS

1 WHOLE EGG

SALT

FOR THE GLAZE

JUICE OF ½ LEMON OR 1 TEASPOON OF ALMOND ESSENCE

220 g (8 oz) ICING OR POWDERED SUGAR PER CAKE

TO MAKE THE POPPY-SEED FILLING

Place the seeds into a saucepan and add the milk. Heat gently for 10 minutes, stirring occasionally, then leave to soak overnight.

Next morning drain off the liquid and grind the seeds in a food processor on the finest setting until they turn to a paste – not too smooth, though, as the paste needs to retain some crunch. Melt the butter and add this to the paste with the vanilla sugar, chopped almonds, walnuts, the lemon zest, and a few drops of almond essence. Stir together well.

Beat the egg whites to form peaks and fold them in.

TO MAKE THE CAKE

Preheat the oven to 180°C (350°F).

Beat the butter, sugar, and egg yolks in a bowl until creamy. Stir in the milk. Mix the flour and yeast separately, then add to the bowl with the sultanas (golden raisins). Add a pinch of salt and stir it all together.

Cover with a clean tea towel or dishcloth and leave in a warm place to prove for an hour or so. The cake mixture should double in size.

Roll out on a floured board into a rectangle about 1 cm (½ in) thick. (If you are making 2 cakes divide the dough into two and roll out two rectangles.)

Generously spread the cake dough with the poppy-seed filling then roll up the cake lengthways like a Swiss roll. Seal the ends by squeezing the pastry together so the filling won't fall out as the cake cooks. Whisk the whole egg and use it to paint the top and sides of the cake with a pastry or basting brush so it has a smooth shiny surface when baked. Wrap a sheet of baking paper around the roll to stop it growing in the oven. Bake for 45 minutes.

TO MAKE THE GLAZE

Put the sugar in a bowl and slowly add the almond essence or lemon juice until you have a smooth runny glaze (*lukier*). Pour over the cake before it has cooled.

A Parable of the Poppy

On a poppy seed is a tiny house,
Dogs bark at the poppy-seed moon,
And never, never do those poppy-seed dogs
Imagine that somewhere there is a world much larger.

The Earth is a seed – and really no more,
While other seeds are planets and stars.
And even if there were a hundred thousand,
Each might have a house and a garden.

All in a poppy head. The poppy grows tall,
The children run by and the poppy sways.
And in the evening, under the rising moon,
Dogs bark somewhere, now loudly, now softly.

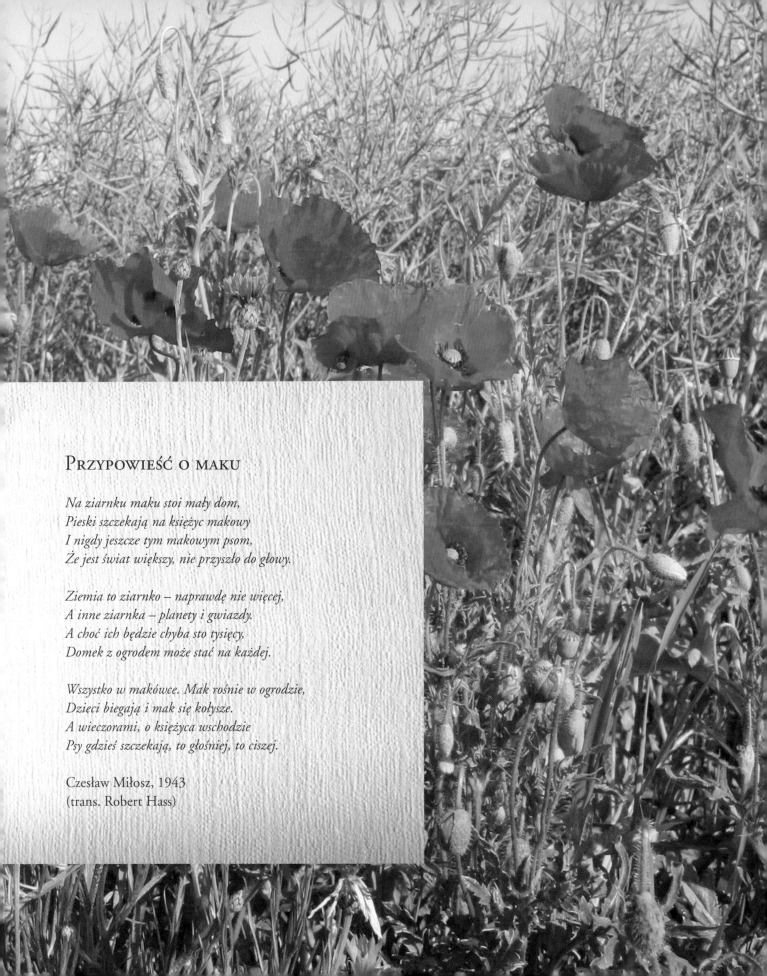

Przypowieść o maku

Na ziarnku maku stoi mały dom,
Pieski szczekają na księżyc makowy
I nigdy jeszcze tym makowym psom,
Że jest świat większy, nie przyszło do głowy.

Ziemia to ziarnko – naprawdę nie więcej,
A inne ziarnka – planety i gwiazdy.
A choć ich będzie chyba sto tysięcy,
Domek z ogrodem może stać na każdej.

Wszystko w makówce. Mak rośnie w ogrodzie,
Dzieci biegają i mak się kołysze.
A wieczorami, o księżyca wschodzie
Psy gdzieś szczekają, to głośniej, to ciszej.

Czesław Miłosz, 1943
(trans. Robert Hass)

Julia's Summer Fruit Liqueurs

Birthdays, "name days", or special family gatherings were always a good excuse to try Julia's latest homemade, alcoholic concoctions. Her speciality was creating fruit liqueurs (*nalewki*) made from blackcurrants, sour cherries, or any fruits she could find in our garden. She drowned the fruit in sugar and spiritus – a form of rectified spirit that is nearly pure alcohol. I clearly remember the intense, sweet flavour on the tip of my tongue: I must have once licked the empty liqueur glasses when no-one was looking.

To mark each vintage of her *nalewki*, Julia tied different coloured threads round the necks of her bottles, as if awarding stars to a fine cognac. She hid them in remote corners of the house, telling the family there was nothing left until next summer. The men soon learned that the best way to coax some out of her was to criticise the latest vintage, saying it wasn't as good as last year's. Provoked, Julia would proudly produce the "last" bottle, miraculously found in an abandoned piano, cupboard, or wardrobe, to prove them wrong. But before anyone was allowed the smallest drop, Julia would sample the liqueur herself, sipping it slowly, checking its colour, enjoying centre stage and the impatience of her thirsty audience. Finally the bottle would be placed on the table, to be shared around immediately and the empty flask recycled for next season.

30

Rose Petal Jam

ABOVE Family meal in the farmhouse kitchen. From left to right, Beata's mother Lidia, Aunt Sabina, Uncle Jasiu, great grandmother Julia, grandmother Józefa, and Beata.

Sour Cherry Liqueur § NALEWKA WIŚNIOWA

The active ingredient in *nalewka* is Polish spiritus – a form of rectified alcohol repeatedly distilled until it is very strong – up to 95% proof. Obtainable in fine liquor stores, it is not a good idea to try drinking this undiluted!

The recipe works for many fruits – plums, blackcurrants, blackberries – and makes around 2 litres (a little over 4 pints) of roughly 20% proof *nalewka* that will last for at least two years. You may need to adjust the amount of sugar according to the ripeness and type of fruit, e.g. if using a sweet or sour variety of cherry. And you can add more or less spiritus to vary its strength. Friends are usually very willing to help taste and give advice.

ENOUGH FOR 30–40 SHOTS

3 kg (6 lb 10 oz) STONED OR PITTED SOUR CHERRIES

2 HANDFULS SOUR CHERRIES WITH STONES/SEEDS

2 kg (4 lb 7 oz) CASTER (SUPERFINE) SUGAR

500 ml–1 l (17–34 fl oz) SPIRITUS (80% PROOF)

Put all the fruit in a large glass jar and stir in the sugar. Cover with a clean cloth and leave for a week. During this time the cherries will release their juice.

After a week add the spiritus. The quantity that you add depends on how strong you would like your drink to be: 1 litre (34 fl oz) spiritus makes a good strong drink.

Mix in the spiritus well then leave to settle for half an hour. Now sieve through a fine strainer into bottles, and the liqueur is ready to drink. Keep the leftover fruit – the cherries with stones will still be intact – in the fridge and use for an (adults only) dessert.

32

Mint Liqueur § LIKIER MIĘTOWY

A syrupy after-dinner liqueur (pictured on page 35).

ENOUGH FOR 25 SHOTS

1 LARGE BUNCH PEPPERMINT, LEAVES ONLY, STALKS REMOVED

500 ml (17 fl oz) WATER

500 g (1 lb 2 oz) CASTER (SUPERFINE) SUGAR

200 ml (7 fl oz) SPIRITUS (80% PROOF)

Simmer the mint leaves in the water with the sugar for 10 minutes to make a thick syrup.

Strain the liquid into a bowl. Allow to cool, then stir in the spiritus.

Strain again into sterilized bottles and leave for a week before drinking.

This makes about a litre (roughly 2 pints) of liqueur.

Pepper Vodka § PIEPRZÓWKA

Pepper vodka has long been used as a tonic for an unsettled stomach. 19th-century Polish migrants to America carried homemade pepper vodka to treat seasickness while crossing the rough Atlantic waters. In my family you were always allowed a sip for purely medicinal purposes, unless you had been in good health for a long time, in which case you could have some anyway.

This recipe uses vodka rather than spiritus. You can use pink or black peppercorns but white peppercorns seem to give the strongest aroma.

ENOUGH FOR 15–20 SHOTS

5 TABLESPOONS WHITE PEPPERCORNS

500 ml (17 fl oz) VODKA

Put the peppercorns in a sealable jar and pour over the vodka. Seal the jar and shake. Leave to stand for a couple of days.

Serve, chilled, in shot glasses. You can filter out the peppercorns if you wish, though they do look pretty in the bottom of the glass.

Half a German farmhouse…

Józefa loved the south-western corner of Poland where we lived, but she did not grow up there. She came from Lwów, hundreds of kilometres to the east, from the *kresy* or borderlands. After the Second World War, the *kresy* became part of the USSR. Poland's borders moved to the west, and so did my family. Józefa had lost her husband in the war. He was only 30; she 26. A young widow, she set off to start a new life on the other side of the country with her parents Julia and Dimitri, her sisters Janina and Izabela, her six-year-old son Jasiu, and her two-year-old daughter Lidia – my mother.

The family of seven were resettled in Lower Silesia, a part of Germany before the war but by then a part of Poland. They were offered half a farmhouse in a remote country village in the foothills of the Karkanosze Mountains. There was only one obstacle – a German family was still living in the other half of the farmhouse, waiting to be resettled farther west themselves, and they would all have to share together. And so two families, Germans and Poles, meant to be sworn enemies, sat down and ate dinner together. With the odd bullet still flying through the mountain skies, the rational human need for friendship and acceptance took over from all the irrationality of war.

The German owner had elaborate machinery for making wheels and wooden barrels. Unable to take the equipment with him, he taught my great-grandfather how to use it. It was some consolation to the German family after they left that Dimitri would be able to make use of their tools to make barrels, wheels, and crates for the new villagers.

For a while barrel-making gave our family a small source of barter income – until the new communist government pronounced Dimitri a *kułak*, or capitalist, for making a profit and closed him down for good. Proud Dimitri never worked again, from 1948 until his death in 1965. The family were then supported entirely by Józefa. She got a job in the village as a chef cooking in an old German hunting lodge that had been converted into a holiday resort. Meanwhile her parents, Julia and Dimitri, planted rows of vegetables and fruit in the garden around the house, always grumbling about the poor mountain soil. They could not forget the large watermelons and pumpkins that had sprouted so easily back home in the Ukrainian fields.

FAR LEFT Grandmother Józefa (left) with her sister Janina as young girls back home in the *kresy*. LEFT Józefa (left) and her sister (right), with Józefa's husband Rudi and his little brother just before the Second World War, in Brzeżany, near Lwów.

Mushroom Missions

One of my most important summer missions was to patrol the forest with other village children looking for precious wild mushrooms. If it had rained the previous night, there might be new-grown mushrooms out there somewhere, hidden under an oak or pine tree. First thing in the morning, we would run and look. Of course we kept the precise location of our hunting grounds secret. The most sought-after treasures were the "real" mushrooms – *prawdziwki* – that are similar to Italian porcini mushrooms. Rare and most flavoursome, these were as valuable to us as truffles, and like truffle pigs, we dug through fallen leaves, moss, and pine cones to unearth our trophies.

Before we returned to the village, we loaded our bucket with leaves and acorns, then scattered our few precious mushrooms on top to make it look as if we had a full bucket. Impressed villagers asked as we strutted past where we had found all the mushrooms. We turned and pointed vaguely to some mountains about five kilometres away. If you were lucky enough to find any *prawdziwki* you knew that once dried they could be used to add a delicious flavour to the family's meals for the rest of the year. That was a secret worth keeping.

Once home Julia inspected my share of the haul carefully to filter out poisonous or hallucinogenic undesirables. Aha! She would snatch a

OPPOSITE LEFT Józefa's recipe for marinated mushrooms.

Rose Petal Jam

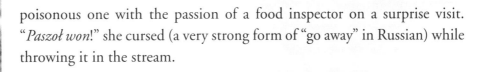

poisonous one with the passion of a food inspector on a surprise visit. "*Paszoł won!*" she cursed (a very strong form of "go away" in Russian) while throwing it in the stream.

We had been taught when very young how to pick a mushroom by breaking or cutting the stem so as not to damage the root. To clean it we had to remove each pine needle, leaf, and twig carefully by hand. Any imperfectly shaped mushrooms were used with added fresh cream to make a potent sauce to adorn some pasta or meat but the best would all be stored for future use. Using a needle, Julia would thread strong cotton through the stalks and soon garlands of mushrooms would be hanging out to dry by an open attic window. On hot summer nights the aroma of mushrooms slowly dehydrating in our roof would seep through the walls of the house, infusing our dreams with rainbow colours.

43

Pickled Mushrooms § GRZYBY MARYNOWANE

Fresh mushrooms can be preserved for many months by drying – either by leaving them out in the sun on trays until completely dry or placing in a warm oven with an open door for a few hours, as my great-grandmother Julia used to do. They can also be preserved in jars by pickling for up to a couple of years. Pickled mushrooms make a fine appetizer, perhaps with a shot of vodka, a kind of Polish antipasto. Here's Józefa's special pickling method, which I found in one of her old recipe notebooks.

ENOUGH FOR 10 MEDIUM-SIZED JARS

1 kg (2 lb 3 oz) SMALL FRESH MUSHROOMS, MIXED VARIETIES, STALKS PRESERVED

½ TEASPOON SALT

1.25 l (42 fl oz) WATER

100 ml (3 fl oz) WHITE VINEGAR

3 BAY LEAVES

6 GRAINS ALL SPICE

1 TEASPOON SUGAR

10 BLACK PEPPERCORNS

Wash the mushrooms carefully and place in a saucepan with half a teaspoon of salt. Cover with water and bring to the boil. As soon as the water boils, drain the mushrooms and set aside. The idea is to sterilise the mushrooms for a moment, not to cook them.

Prepare the pickling liquid by placing all the ingredients (except the mushrooms) in a saucepan and bringing to the boil. Simmer gently for 10 minutes. Allow to cool to room temperature.

Put the mushrooms into sterilized jars then fill up with the pickling liquid. Seal the jars tightly (see page 18) and store in a cool place.

44

Rose Petal Jam

RIGHT Beata (left), aged six, heading off to pick mushrooms with two friends.

Józefa's Rissoles with Wild Mushrooms and Buckwheat

ZRAZY MIELONE W SOSIE GRZYBOWYM Z KASZĄ GRYCZANĄ

If there was no-one game enough to hunt for the "real" wild mushrooms in the forest you could buy them at the local market. This recipe can also be made with dried Italian porcini mushrooms. The buckwheat makes a great side dish to soak up the sauce.

ENOUGH FOR 4–6

500 g (1 lb 2 oz) BUCKWHEAT GROATS

1 TEASPOON SALT

3 OR 4 DRIED WILD OR "REAL" MUSHROOMS OR DRIED PORCINI

1 SMALL ONION, CHOPPED

500 g (1 lb 2 oz) MINCED BEEF

2 TABLESPOONS PLAIN (ALL-PURPOSE) FLOUR

3–4 TABLESPOONS LIGHT OR SINGLE CREAM

HANDFUL CHOPPED PARSLEY

Put the buckwheat in a saucepan and cover with boiling water. Stir in a teaspoon of salt. Simmer gently on a medium heat until the grains have opened and are soft, and most of the water has been absorbed. Leave to cool.

If you are using dried mushrooms, place them in a saucepan, cover with cold water, and soak for 1 hour.

Bring the mushrooms to the boil and cook them gently with a pinch of salt for 15 minutes. Remove the mushrooms (keeping the cooking liquid), cut into thick slices, and set aside.

Mix the chopped onion with the minced beef and shape into small round rissoles, the size of golf balls. Season with pepper and salt, then roll in a little flour and place in a saucepan.

Add half the reserved cooking liquid and a little more fresh water so the rissoles are just covered. Gently simmer for 15 minutes, then drain.

Mix a tablespoon of flour with a tablespoon of the stock into a smooth and runny paste. Slowly add it back to the stock in the saucepan and stir well over a low heat for a few minutes. Once thickened, add the cream.

Add the rissoles to the sauce, along with the sliced mushrooms, and simmer over a medium heat for a further 5 minutes.

Stir in a handful of chopped parsley before serving with the buckwheat and slices of pickled cucumber.

Rose Petal Jam

Pasta with Mushrooms and Cabbage

Łazanki

Łazanki is a traditional Polish dish – a tasty combination of pasta and cabbage. Packets of *łazanki* – small squares of dried egg pasta – are obtainable from most delis, but you can use any shape of small-sized egg pasta instead if you prefer, or make your own. My great-grandmother Julia would add some fried bacon, or diced and fried ham, just before serving for a non-vegetarian, more hearty alternative.

ENOUGH FOR 2

½ MEDIUM-SIZED WHITE CABBAGE

300 g (11 oz) MUSHROOMS, SLICED

1 LARGE ONION, CHOPPED

500 g (1 lb 2 oz) ŁAZANKI PASTA

1 TABLESPOON OLIVE OIL

FOR HOMEMADE PASTA

500 g (1 lb 2 oz) SUPERFINE PLAIN (ALL-PURPOSE) FLOUR

2 EGGS

PINCH SALT

Cut the cabbage into 2 and boil in salted water for 10 minutes or until soft. Remove, drain, and shred.

Cook the pasta in boiling water according to instructions on the packet until it is just *al dente*, then drain.

In a big frying pan or wok fry the chopped onion and sliced mushrooms in the olive oil. Add the pasta and cabbage, tossing everything together with some salt and pepper and serve straight away.

TO MAKE YOUR OWN ŁAZANKI PASTA SQUARES...

It is best to use what the Italians call "double zero" (00) flour.

Using your hands mix the ingredients in a large bowl to make a pastry dough.

Roll out the dough as thinly as possible, adding 1 or 2 tablespoons of water if necessary to make the pastry easier to handle, or more flour if it gets too sticky. Cut into 1 cm (½ in) squares.

Fresh pasta like this will take less time to cook than dried pre-brought pasta – only a minute or 2 in boiling water.

50

Rose Petal Jam

52

Rose Petal Jam

My Great-grandparents Julia and Dimitri

My great-grandparents, Julia and Dimitri, were as devoted and loyal to each other as a pair of storks that mate for life. However Julia and Dimitri had married without their parents' approval. Polish Catholic Julia and Russian Orthodox Dimitri were born in the same village, in the *kresy*, Poland's eastern borderlands. According to family legend, one snowy winter's night they eloped to another village about seven kilometres away. They returned the next day husband and wife, wrapped in snow-covered furs, in a horse drawn sleigh.

After 50 years of marriage they did not like to be separated, even for a day. Whenever Julia went into the local town, Jelenia Góra, to go shopping Dimitri would wait for hours at the bus stop for her return. Banned from his barrel-making business he sat on the bench by the road and watched other villagers walking to the nearby collective farm. He was proud of his uncompromising anti-communist views, an outcast *kułak*, sentenced to years of boredom and poverty. There were only two buses a day, and when the afternoon bus returned with his bride, he would greet her with the warmest embrace and carry her shopping the 100 metres up to the house.

ABOVE Portrait of Julia and Dimitri. RIGHT The old German farmhouse in 1945.

I was only four when Dimitri died. Julia put on the black dress she would wear for the rest of her life and sat in the upstairs kitchen window staring at the mountains and the cemetery on the edge of the village. I now slept in her room, in Dimitri's old cedar bed. The village children used to tease me that Dimitri's ghost would visit us in the night. I was terrified, but the ghost never appeared. Perhaps he didn't like the sharp light of Julia's bedside reading lamp. Julia spoke five languages and read long into every night. But whenever I woke each morning, her bed was already neatly made up. The smell of hot cocoa would be drifting in from the kitchen, along with the reassuring sound of the day's weather forecast on the radio.

Julia devoured books. When she had exhausted all the local libraries she started on my textbooks, then instruction manuals, and, eventually, in her dotage, the phonebook. With the kilograms of flour, sugar, and tea we carried home on the bus each week there was always a new book for Julia, her daily bread. She politely accepted whatever we bought her, even if she'd read it before. Her nose touched the opening sentence and lips whispered *dziękuję* – thank you.

One day, when she was 88 years old, she put on her Sunday best, lay down on her bed and quietly died, without fuss or drama, as if anxious not to spoil our day. I remember seeing her lying there, perfectly still in her pressed black dress, clutching her black rosary. I thought: she has finally run out of books to read. Now she could join her beloved Dimitri in the village's tiny cemetery.

ABOVE RIGHT "Helenka with a mug" by Stanisław Wyspiański, 1902, from the collection of the National Gallery in Kraków.

55

Rose Petal Jam

The icon of the Black Madonna is the most precious treasure of the monastery of Jasna Góra, in Częstochowa. For nearly 500 years it has been a symbol of Polish faith. In an increasingly secular Europe, Częstochowa is still swamped with pilgrims who, in medieval tradition, choose to make their way there on foot and shuffle on their knees past the Black Madonna.

THE BLACK MADONNA

My great-grandmother Julia had a postcard-sized holy picture of the "Black Madonna" – a medieval image of the Virgin Mary, portrayed with dark skin. She carried it around as a marker in her prayer book. During mass, Julia often dropped her picture while kneeling in the middle of prayer, her eyes tightly shut and hands wired together with a black crystal rosary. Not wanting to interrupt her conversation with God, I would dive under the pews to retrieve it for her, crawling along the floor in my white gloves, smudging them on the black polish of worshippers' shiny shoes. I would finally emerge, holding the picture above my head like a successful pearl fisher. She nodded thankfully from underneath her black scarf, all the while continuing to whisper her prayer.

 *Pierogi* POLISH "RAVIOLI"

My great-grandfather Dimitri made a huge wooden board (*stolnica*) for his daughter, my grandmother Józefa, just for making *pierogi*. It was a very generous size, covering half the kitchen table, and had beautifully carved raised edges so you could roll out pastry dough without spilling flour onto the floor. When Józefa put it on the table and started to sprinkle it with flour, I knew she would be making my favourite meal – *pierogi ruskie*.

This recipe makes about 120 *pierogi*, which sounds a lot, but if you have a big family or more than a couple of hungry friends they will all soon disappear. Any leftovers are delicious re-fried in a little butter the next day.

TO MAKE THE PASTRY FOR 120 PIEROGI

1 kg (2 lb 3 oz) PLAIN (ALL-PURPOSE) FLOUR

125 g (4 ½ oz) UNSALTED BUTTER

500 ml (17 fl oz) WARM WATER

Soften the butter in the microwave or by leaving it out of the fridge for a while. Pile the flour onto a large wooden board, then slowly work in the butter with your fingers.

Mix in the warm water, little by little, to make an elastic, soft dough. Place it in a bowl and cover with a clean tea or dish towel so it doesn't dry out while you are preparing the filling.

Roll out a lump of pastry dough on the wooden board – not too thick or thin – 3 mm (⅛ in) is good. Using an inverted tumbler, cut out circles about 8 cm (3 ½ in) in diameter and lay them on a floured wooden board, again covering with a tea or dish towel until you are ready to fill them.

Rose Petal Jam

Pierogi with Cheese and Potato ("Russian")

§ PIEROGI RUSKIE

This variant of *pierogi* with a traditional cheese and potato filling comes from the *kresy* in the east where my great-grandparents Julia and Dimitri grew up. "Farm" cheese is a mild, white, dry-curd cottage cheese sold in blocks in supermarkets. You can eat *pierogi* with a little melted butter drizzled on top and sour cream on the side, or some chopped grilled bacon.

MAKES 120 *PIEROGI*

FOR THE FILLING

3 kg (6 lb 10 oz) POTATOES

3 LARGE WHITE ONIONS, CHOPPED

OLIVE OIL OR BUTTER FOR FRYING

1.2 kg (2 lb 10 oz) "FARM" CHEESE

½ TEASPOON SALT

Peel then boil the potatoes in salted water until tender; drain and mash.

Dice the onions and fry in some oil or butter until soft. Crumble the cheese and mix with the fried onion and the cooled mash. Hold back a little fried onion for garnishing. Add salt and pepper to taste.

Take the prepared circles of pastry dough (see page 59) and place a teaspoon of filling on each. Fold each in half and carefully close it, crimping the pastry together with your fingers so you end up with little semi-circles. (You can buy a simple, hinged utensil to do this.)

Put the *pierogi* into a big pot of boiling water with half a teaspoon of salt. The moment they float to the top (which will not take more than a minute) take them out carefully with a slotted spoon to allow them to drain and serve with the reserved fried onion or some melted butter and sour cream.

62

Pierogi with Beef § PIEROGI Z MIĘSEM

This was the recipe my grandmother used when she tried to encourage me to eat some red meat: I was too young to tackle a steak with a knife and fork. She minced the beef with vegetables and hid it in a yummy pastry envelope. Sometimes she mixed beef *pierogi* in amongst my favourite cheese *pierogi* – they were so flavoursome they eventually became my second favourite. Boiled *pierogi* are nice and chewy, but frying them (once cooked) in a little butter makes for a delicious snack or appetiser, perhaps with a strong Polish beer.

MAKES 120 *PIEROGI*

FOR THE FILLING

2 ONIONS, FINELY CHOPPED

2 CARROTS, PEELED AND ROUGHLY CHOPPED

2 kg (4 lb 7 oz) BEEF RIBS

½ BUNCH CURLY LEAF PARSLEY, CHOPPED

500 ml (17 fl oz) WATER

2 STALE BREAD ROLLS

2 TABLESPOONS OLIVE OIL

1 TABLESPOON BUTTER

Preheat the oven to 160°C (320°F).

Fry half the onion, the parsley, and the carrots in a heavy bottomed, oven-proof saucepan.

Add the water and beef ribs, then put the lid on the pan and bake in the oven for 1 hour.

Allow the pan to cool a little before removing the bones and discarding them, taking care to keep all the meat. Soften the bread rolls in some water, squeeze them dry, then stir into the mixture so they soak up the thick gravy. Put the mix through a mincer.

Fry the remaining onion in a pan with the butter until it is translucent. Stir in the minced beef mixture and fry for a few more minutes. Season with salt and pepper.

Prepare the circles of pastry dough as in the previous recipe (on page 59) and put a teaspoon of the minced beef mixture on each.

Fold them in half and carefully close them, crimping the pastry together with your fingers so you end up with little semi-circles. Put the *pierogi* into a big pot of boiling water with half a teaspoon of salt. The moment they float to the top (which will not take more than a minute) take them out carefully with a slotted spoon to allow them to drain.

If desired, fry for a couple of minutes in a little butter. You can also add some chopped bacon.

65

Rose Petal Jam

Pierogi with Buckwheat and Cheese

ʃ PIEROGI Z KASZĄ GRYCZANĄ

We often ate this type of vegetarian *pierogi* on a Friday when Poles traditionally don't eat meat. ("Farm" or "farm-style" cheese is a mild, white, dry curd cottage cheese sold in blocks at supermarkets and delis.)

MAKES 120 *PIEROGI*

FOR THE FILLING

500 g (1 lb 2 oz) BUCKWHEAT GROATS

1 TEASPOON SALT

250 g (9 oz) "FARM" CHEESE

½ ONION, CHOPPED AND FRIED

Place the buckwheat in a large saucepan and cover with boiling water. Add the salt and bring it back to the boil. Turn off the heat, cover, and leave for 10 minutes for the buckwheat to soften. (Different brands of buckwheat may have different cooking times – check the packet. The grains will absorb all the water, but should remain separate and not stick together like porridge.) Once softened, set aside to cool.

Break up the cheese with a fork and mix it well with the fried onion and buckwheat. Season with pepper and salt.

Make the pastry dough as per the recipe on page 59.

Let the filling mixture cool a little before placing a teaspoonful on each circle of pastry.

Seal the *pierogi* (see page 62) and then cook in a large saucepan with lots of salted boiling water, stirring carefully to prevent them sticking together. Remove the *pierogi* when they float to the top after a minute or so.

Drain well in a strainer and serve with chopped fried bacon or melted butter.

The good German doctor

There were three headstones in the far corner of the village cemetery inscribed with German names. I always wondered why these graves were in the Polish cemetery, rather than in the old German one behind, with its elaborate Gothic inscriptions on granite tombs guarded by sorrowful stone angels.

My grandmother Józefa explained that these were the graves of a German doctor, his nurse, and his housekeeper who had stayed on after the War, when Lower Silesia became Polish. When the Germans left Dr Deinert remained, treating newly arrived Polish families without asking for payment. He tried to speak their language and showed Poles love and kindness at a time when such humanity must have been at odds with his own survival. He was often referred to as "the good German doctor". My mother and uncle remembered that there was a white rocking chair in the shape of a swan to play on in his waiting room. Dr Deinert was the first to diagnose my grandmother's rheumatic heart disease that would claim her life some years later.

In 1948 Dr Deinert and his staff were murdered; the circumstances remain a mystery to this day. Over a thousand people attended the funeral and it was decided that all three should be buried in the village's Polish cemetery in recognition of their dedication to the Polish community. Over the years these graves have always been well kept, with flowers and candles: when I last visited I was amazed to see a lit candle on Dr Deinert's grave. I realized that he is still a part of the village's history, remembered for his good deeds by a new generation of Poles.

When walking through the fields with my grandmother we often collected two bunches of wildflowers to take to the cemetery – one for Józefa's father, Dimitri, and one for the "good German doctor". Even though I was only four, his story inspired me to announce to my grandmother that I too was going to be a "good doctor". It's a promise I still try to keep. Sometimes when I struggle to understand a new patient who has recently migrated to Australia and doesn't speak much English, I think of Dr Deinert. I imagine him smiling at my three-year-old Polish mother, asking her, in German, to stick out her tongue.

High School in Jelenia Góra

By the time I was old enough for school, I moved to live with my parents in Jelenia Góra and only stayed with my grandmother in her village during holidays. Józefa often came to cook for us all in our city apartment. She would arrive laden with a big wicker basket full of village supplies: large jars of dark amber honey and a block of farm cheese that she had bartered for a bag of Julia's poppy seeds. Precisely counted blades of chives from her garden were rolled in baking paper so they wouldn't crush on the bus. Precious eggs were individually wrapped in old newspapers that celebrated the economic success of communism.

Our Lyceum looked like a castle, a five-storey building with wide staircases and corridors, built high up on a hill overlooking the town. The school had a gravitas that said "learning is a serious business". I came to appreciate the high standard of teaching here and will always feel gratitude to my Polish teachers. Thanks to all Józefa's love and encouragement and my parents' support my final exams went well and I won a place to study medicine in Wrocław. As fate had it, I would finish my studies on the other side of the world, in Sydney.

Józefa's "Daisy" Eggs *§ JAJKA W SKORUPKACH*

In my last week of high school, before I went off to sit the exams that would determine whether I had any hope of becoming a doctor, Józefa made a special trip to our apartment in Jelenia Góra. She came so she could cook me "Daisy Eggs" for breakfast. This is a popular way to serve eggs in Poland – the eggs are boiled, then chopped with herbs and butter, and served in their shells. Józefa arranged them on the plate in a daisy pattern – hence her nickname for one of my childhood favourites.

Józefa returned the used egg shells to the village for Julia to feed back to the chickens. Julia would first pulverise the shells in her bronze mortar, especially if they had been imprinted with communist slogans from their newspaper wrapping.

3 FRESH EGGS (OR AS MANY AS THE FAMILY CAN EAT)

1 TABLESPOON DILL, PARSLEY, AND CHIVES, FINELY CHOPPED

BUTTER FOR FRYING

74

Hard boil the eggs for 5 minutes, then run them under cold water for a moment so they are not too hot to handle. Using a sharp knife cut the eggs (still in their shells) lengthwise into 2.

Scoop out the yolks and whites, keeping the shells intact. Chop the egg roughly and mix with whatever herbs you have to hand – dill, parsley, chives. Add salt and pepper to season and carefully replace the mixture in the egg shells without breaking them.

Fry face down in a little butter for a few minutes until lightly brown. Arrange like daisy petals on a plate and serve with fresh bread for breakfast, lunch, or a snack when studying.

Moving Away

In 1981 I left Poland with my young brother and parents for a new life in Australia. My grandmother Józefa was too sick to join us on our journey though we planned for her to come later when she had recovered. I only found out she had died when we reached Sydney, nearly a year later. Her passing kept me away from Poland. I could not imagine returning without her there.

Years went by as I lived among the silvery eucalypts, blue skies, and friendliness of Australia. But I never forgot the country I grew up in. Sometimes when the wind blew in the two tall gums outside our Sydney terrace they sounded like the linden trees next to Józefa's old farmhouse. I started reading 19th-century Polish Romantic poetry, composed at a time when, partitioned between its neighbours, Poland had ceased to exist. Exiles in Paris had written nostalgically about the country they had lost. Having lived 20,000 kilometres away for two decades, poetry that had been meaningless to me at school in Poland now moved me to tears.

It was definitely time to go back.

My Song (II)

For the land where a scrap of bread is picked up
From the ground out of reverence
For Heaven's gifts... I am homesick, Lord!

For the land where it's a great travesty
To harm a stork's nest in a pear tree,
For storks serve us all... I am homesick, Lord!

Moja Piosenka (II)

Do kraju tego, gdzie kruszynę chleba
Podnoszą z ziemi przez uszanowanie
Dla darów Nieba... Tęskno mi, Panie..

Do kraju tego, gdzie winą jest dużą
Popsować gniazdo na gruszy bocianie,
Bo wszystkim służą... Tęskno mi, Panie..

Cyprian Kamil Norwid, 1871
(trans. Walter Whipple)

Return of the Stork

I had been away for more than twenty years when one day my husband Simon came home with two tickets to Poland. I had only a few days to get ready. We flew to Kraków, rented a car and set off for my grandmother's village. I felt apprehensive returning after so long; what would the place be like without my grandmother? As we drove west across southern Poland, we wound down the windows to let in the smell of the summer. I tried to relax by teaching Simon to sing Polish songs.

I saw Józefa from the car window everywhere, always far away, crossing a street or a meadow, a glimpse of her behind a lacy window curtain or at the back of a tram as it shrank into the distance. My psychology textbook would call it "unresolved grief" but I would diagnose "undying love".

We soon reached the village with its few dozen cottages clustered along a fast-moving mountain stream. And where the stream turned under a stone bridge stood the house of my childhood. Perhaps smaller than I remember, but still magnificent and proud like my great grandfather Dimitri in his army uniform. The house had been repainted and re-roofed for the next century of hot summers and cold winters, with new foundations to withstand the footsteps of a new generation of young children.

My uncle Jasiu was waiting outside, with my aunt Sabina and cousin Maciek and his wife Małgosia. As we drew near they started waving and running towards the car in case I forgot to stop and drove off for another twenty years! We were welcomed with open hearts. Simon was swept up in all the tears, hugs and kisses, and felt immediately included into a family who seemed to have missed him without ever having met him before. It was a magic moment when he was christened "Szymon" and started to surrender some of his Anglo Saxon cool for Slavic over-emotion.

The delicious homecoming feast had to wait until I had said hello to someone to whom I had never said a final farewell. We tried to press the creases out of clothes, bought flowers and candles at the village shop and walked through the summer evening to the little cemetery lined with pine trees. I had to close my eyes when I saw Józefa's name written on a

tombstone. I sat on the seat nearby with Simon and thought how much I would have liked to have had just a few minutes with her, to hug her, to smell her chamomile face cream, and bury my head in her flowery dress. I wanted to tell her how much I missed her and how much I still loved her, that I had kept my promise to study and travel, and how much I loved my work, my children and my husband. I know she would have approved of Simon and would have spoiled him with her cooking. I could almost hear her say: "He's alright. He can leave his shoes under your bed".

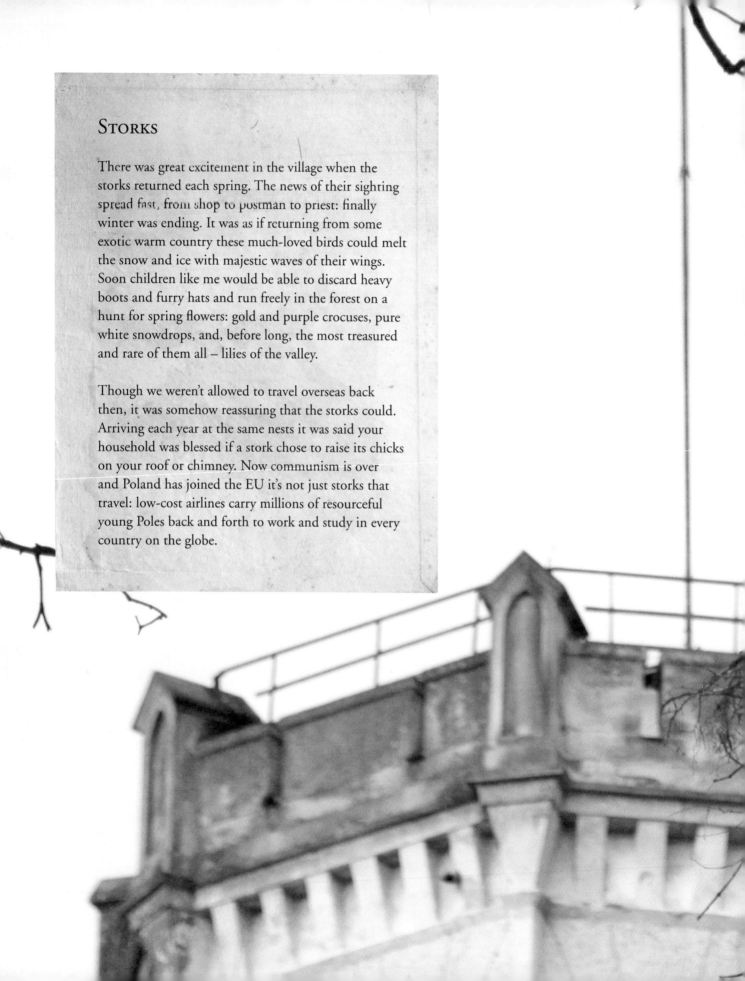

Storks

There was great excitement in the village when the storks returned each spring. The news of their sighting spread fast, from shop to postman to priest: finally winter was ending. It was as if returning from some exotic warm country these much-loved birds could melt the snow and ice with majestic waves of their wings. Soon children like me would be able to discard heavy boots and furry hats and run freely in the forest on a hunt for spring flowers: gold and purple crocuses, pure white snowdrops, and, before long, the most treasured and rare of them all – lilies of the valley.

Though we weren't allowed to travel overseas back then, it was somehow reassuring that the storks could. Arriving each year at the same nests it was said your household was blessed if a stork chose to raise its chicks on your roof or chimney. Now communism is over and Poland has joined the EU it's not just storks that travel: low-cost airlines carry millions of resourceful young Poles back and forth to work and study in every country on the globe.

Prussian Palaces

Now that I was back, I didn't want to leave the village. The local trees, the river, and the meadows became my world – all I needed to be happy. My universe was contracting, so Simon dragged me off to explore neighbouring towns. We wandered slowly through narrow cobblestone streets, dark and cool despite the midday sun, saying hello to languorous cats guarding window baskets full of flowers. We tiptoed into quiet churches, trying to find our way through a thick fog of incense. We slipped into the last row of pews, which often squeaked with surprise as we sat down, making praying heads turn towards us.

Every village in the foothills around Śnieżka seems to have one, two, or three palaces under lengthy renovation. Some are meticulously restored as private homes or hotels. Many still await loving owners. It was Prince Wilhelm, brother of the Prussian king, who started the fashion for palace building here. In 1830 he constructed a turreted chateau with moat and drawbridge in Fischbach, a short walk from where our family farmhouse is today. Then King William III himself set about renovating the old castle in nearby Erdmannsdorf (now Mysłakowice) as his official summer residence. It was reputed to have a view fit for an emperor of snow-capped Śnieżka – the highest peak in the mountains. Soon every Prussian nobleman just had to have a country castle near the King's, complete with artificial ruins, romantic temples, and view shafts, like an English country park. Such a princely mountain hideaway full of castles, churches, and gardens would have attracted huge crowds in Tuscany or the Dordogne, but we seemed to be the only tourists.

A Musical Treasure Trove

One day I took Simon to Krzeszów Abbey. This grand monastery is hidden away in a remote village, far from major roads and cities. I did not tell Simon about the Baroque splendours awaiting us inside that I remembered so well from school excursions long ago.

We stood outside for some time admiring the stony facades and sculptures around the entrance. Finally we stepped into the basilica. Heaven must look like that... all light and air, with colourful, swirling paintings on the ceilings and gilded altars, pulpits and balconies, crystal chandeliers, and white marble angels holding up a massive silver organ on their shoulders.

Such bewildering Baroque exuberance is nearly impossible to comprehend in today's times of ergonomic design and functionality. You can only sit and feel the emotions conveyed in the paintings and sculptures: love, suffering, and death, all around you. The sound of the original 17th-century organ made the atmosphere even more celestial. This organ is one of the best-preserved original instruments in Poland with nearly every component as it was in Bach's time. We were listening to music coming directly from centuries ago. Our spirits were soon floating somewhere up in the vaulted ceiling. It was hard to leave this heavenly church and return to our earthly lives.

Krzeszów Abbey

Krzeszów Abbey was where the original score of Mozart's opera *The Magic Flute* and other important manuscripts were once hidden. Before 1945 Krzeszów was named Grüssau, a remote village deep in south eastern Germany. Five hundred boxes of books and manuscripts from the Prussian State Library in Berlin were stored here during the War to avoid being damaged. They survived intact. In 1945, when the Poles first entered the attic above the church's huge ceiling domes, they opened dusty boxes and made a remarkable discovery: there were original autographed manuscripts of music by Beethoven and Bach and one quarter of all known works by Mozart (including two operas). With Warsaw still in ruins the musical treasure trove was moved to Kraków, where much of it remains today.

Cauliflower Soup ZUPA KALAFIOROWA

Poles eat their main hot meal – *obiad* – as a late lunch each day. When out sightseeing it wouldn't be long before we heard the sound of clinking cutlery coming from open windows as we walked past. The smell of someone's chicken soup or raspberry *kisiel* would fill the air, and we would hurry hungrily home. Polish hospitality had not changed with the times. Our family still believed that a guest must eat all day. Cauliflower soup would be followed by *kluski śląskie*, followed by strawberry roulade, followed by... a snooze on a haystack.

This is a popular summer soup that includes lots of different vegetables, with cauliflower taking the starring role.

SERVES 4

FOR THE STOCK (BOUILLON)

2 CHICKEN WINGS

½ MEDIUM ONION

4 SPRIGS CURLY-LEAF PARSLEY

1 WHOLE CARROT

½ PARSNIP

2 TEASPOONS SALT

FOR THE SOUP

2 CARROTS

½ CELERIAC

1 PARSNIP

5 MEDIUM-SIZED POTATOES

1 LARGE WHITE CAULIFLOWER, BROKEN INTO FLORETS

2 TABLESPOONS FRESH POURING CREAM

1 TABLESPOON CHOPPED FLAT-LEAF PARSLEY

Place the ingredients for the stock in a saucepan and cover with about 2 litres (4 pints) of water. Bring to the boil and simmer for at least an hour.

To make the soup, remove the chicken wings and scoop out half a cup of soup and mix with the cream.

Wash and peel the carrots, celeriac, parsnip, and potatoes and cut them into 1 cm (½ cm) cubes. Add them to the stock and cook for a further 10 minutes, then add the cauliflower.

After 5–10 minutes when the cauliflower has softened a little, stir in the soup/cream mix and the grated cucumbers. Simmer gently for a few more minutes. Season with salt and pepper.

Serve hot with a sprinkling of chopped fresh parsley.

POCZTA

POCZTA

12 5/8 5/ 5/ 8

Aunt Sabina's Silesian Dumplings

§ KLUSKI ŚLĄSKIE

One of the dishes I had missed most was Silesian dumplings (*kluski śląskie*) – a speciality of this part of Poland. Once my kind family knew I was craving these giant gnocchi-like potato dumplings again, everybody started making them. On one occasion we were served *kluski* three times on the same day by different relatives – a true test of Simon's tact and acting skills when trying this dish "for the first time". I don't want to start a fight in the family but no-one cooks them as well as my Aunt Sabina, who often serves them with a Polish goulash and pureed beetroot (*buraczki*, see page 104).

ENOUGH FOR 6

1 kg (2 lb 3 oz) POTATOES
250 g (9 oz) POTATO FLOUR
1 EGG

Peel and boil the potatoes (older, starchier ones are best) until tender, then drain them very well. Put the drained potatoes back on the heat for a few seconds with the lid on, shake, then remove the lid and release all the remaining moisture before mashing the potatoes.

To ensure the correct ratio of potato flour to potato, divide your mash into 4, remove one quarter, and replace with potato flour. Then return the potato you took out and add the egg. Mix it all together with your fingers.

Take a tablespoon of potato mix and roll it in your hands into the shape and size of a golf ball, then make an indent by pressing in with your thumb. Continue until all the potatoe mixture has been used.

Boil the *kluski* in salted water for 2 minutes – they will quickly float to the surface – then drain carefully. They should feel springy when tested with a knife and be chewy to taste, but cooked through.

My Aunt Sabina

I remember playing hide and seek in the woods around the village with my Aunt Sabina and my Uncle Jasiu. I adored Sabina and found her very glamorous. To me she looked like an Italian movie star with her long hair and voluptuous curves. I'm glad my Polish Claudia Cardinale became a chef as lots of our old family recipes were then kept on the boil in her kitchen. She gets four hats for her cooking through four seasons!

When we met again, Sabina seemed oblivious to my being grown up. She was as loving and gentle as I had remembered. She softened my name to "Betuniu" as she used to when we played hide and seek. When we made cabbage rolls together she showed me how to clean the cabbage leaves with a very sharp knife and warned me not to hurt myself, never acknowledging that I might have held a scalpel in my hands before. It was such a warm feeling to remain a child in her loving eyes and made me feel immortal and resilient to grey hair and wrinkles.

Sabina is a talented and generous cook who will spare no money or effort to prepare a six-course meal for the whole family. If someone fails to turn up for her lunch, she sends an envoy with jars and plates of "spare leftovers" for their supper.

ABOVE Aunt Sabina as a teenager. RIGHT Beata, aged five, with Aunt Sabina and Uncle Jasiu playing in the woods.

Polish Beef Goulash *§* GULASZ WOŁOWY

SERVES 6

1kg (2 lb 3 oz) CHUCK OR STEWING STEAK

4 TABLESPOONS PLAIN (ALL-PURPOSE) FLOUR

4 TABLESPOONS OLIVE OIL

2 ONIONS

2 CLOVES GARLIC

2 STICKS CELERY

3 CARROTS

½ BUNCH FLAT-LEAF PARSLEY

1 TABLESPOON DILL

225 g (8 oz) MUSHROOMS

250 ml l (8 fl oz) RED WINE

500 ml (17 fl oz) BEEF STOCK OR BOUILLON

1 TABLESPOON SOUR CREAM

1 TABLESPOON TOMATO CONCENTRATE

1 TABLESPOON SWEET PAPRIKA

Cut the steak into 1 cm (¼ in) cubes. Roll them in flour then brown in 2 tablespoons of olive oil in a heavy-bottomed saucepan or Dutch oven. Remove the meat and set aside.

Chop the parsley stalks, reserving the leaves for later. Dice the onions, celery, and carrots, then sauté on a medium heat in the remaining oil with the finely sliced garlic, and parsley stalks for about 10 minutes. Stir regularly so the vegetables don't stick to the bottom. Add the mushrooms, chopped, and cook for a further 5 minutes.

Add the browned meat to the cooked vegetables. Also add the dill (chopped), the wine, and the stock or bouillon. Simmer on a low heat for 2 hours until the meat is tender, topping up with water if necessary so it does not dry out.

Stir in the sour cream, the tomato concentrate, and some seasoning such as paprika. Add salt and pepper to taste and simmer for a few minutes until the sauce thickens. Stir in the the parsley leaves before serving with *kluski śląskie* (see page 100) or mashed potatoes.

Sweet Pureed Beetroot *§* BURACZKI NA SŁODKO

ENOUGH FOR 4

4 MEDIUM-SIZED FRESH BEETROOT

100g (3 oz) BUTTER

1 TEASPOON PLAIN (ALL-PURPOSE) FLOUR

2 TABLESPOONS LIGHT SOUR CREAM (OPTIONAL)

½ TEASPOON SUGAR

Wash the beetroot, trim the leaves but leave enough stalk on the ends to stop the beetroot releasing all its juice when cooking. Place in a saucepan, cover with water, and bring to the boil. Simmer on a medium heat until soft – about 30 minutes or more. Test if it is ready by seeing if you can easily pierce it with a fork.

Remove from the heat, drain in a sieve or colander, and run cold water over the beetroot to cool it. Peel off the skin using your fingers or a vegetable peeler. Grate the beetroot into a bowl using the finest grater – you are aiming for a mushy, pureed texture.

In a heavy-bottomed saucepan, melt the butter and stir in the flour to make a thin roux. Add the beetroot and fry in the roux, releasing some of its moisture. Season with salt and pepper. For a more luscious mash, add the sugar and the sour cream if desired. Stir well and serve hot.

Samotnia Chalet and the Karkonosze Mountains

108

ABOVE Beata's father Grzegorz (aged seven) sitting above Samotnia chalet and the lake with his mother Marcela. Marcela and her husband George were among the first Polish settlers to arrive in Jelenia Góra from Central Poland in 1945. RIGHT An old postcard of hairpin bend on a road through the Sudety mountains.

The old Sudety mountains surrounded the village and formed the scenic backdrop to the drama of our daily lives. We would gaze at the peaks with a pagan reverence, making predictions about the cloud and fog lifting or descending on our rooftops, or the snow returning to our spring orchards, or the roaring wind threatening all open gates and shutters. The greys and blues of the mountain slopes were reflected in our eyes and souls.

Up there, hidden among the highest peaks, on the edge of a deep, prehistoric glacial lake, was an old wooden chalet called *Samotnia* – "the lonely place". I had been there many times and now wanted Simon to fall in love with this idyllic mountain hideaway too. It took us several hours to climb the narrow track and reach the cliff above the valley. Suddenly we were looking down on a view I remembered so well: I was finally back. I felt the mountains had waited for me unchanged, and was looking forward to sleeping here again, sheltered in their rocky embrace. The last time I had spent a night here was aged seven on a scout trip. I was awoken at midnight, made to dress in my scout uniform, and marched outside into the cold. There, in front of a giant bonfire that sent stars into the sky, I swore my oath of allegiance to the scouts, with the Mountain Spirit – *Duch Gór* – as my witness.

Muzeum
Zabawek i Lalek

Łomnickie
Rozdroże

Jumbo Matic Jan

P

lawiny kam

kocioł

Łomnica

letnia

Symboliczny
Cmentarzyk

Vanishing Borders

The border between Poland and the Czech Republic runs along the summit ridge of the Karkonosze Mountains. Back in communist times, soldiers with rifles were positioned all along the ridge, guarding us from the friendly Czechs on the other side. Standing on top of Śnieżka, the highest peak, they looked like figures from the fairy tales of Hans Christian Andersen, frozen soldiers clutching their machine guns, standing rigid in the gusting wind.

Walking in these mountains during the Cold War was the closest we could ever get to the country's southern border and as children we were briefed how we should always behave: never cross the border nor the guards. But being kids we could not help trying to put a foot over the borderline painted on the granite so we could claim at school next day that we had "been abroad". At a time when very few Poles had a passport or were allowed to travel, that was the true limit of our world.

After an exhausting climb to the top of Śnieżka I felt breathless but happy to conquer it again after 20 years. Today there were no soldiers, no rifles, no signs to mark the borders, just red-and-white stones hidden in amongst the grass and pine needles. I stood on the peak watching other walkers struggle up, only to disperse in all directions, unaware of any national borders. Children, singing at full volume, gave away from which country they had tumbled in: Poland, Czech Republic, Germany. I wished my grandmother Marcela was here with me to see the joyous havoc and feel the exhilaration of how free Poland had become.

VANISHING BORDERS

Return of the Stork

Psalm

Oh, the leaky boundaries of man-made states!
How many clouds float past them with impunity;
how much desert sand shifts from one land to another;
how many mountain pebbles tumble onto foreign soil
in provocative hops!

Need I mention every single bird that flies in the face of frontiers
or alights on the roadblock at the border?
A humble robin – still, its tail resides abroad
while its beak stays home. If that weren't enough, it won't stop bobbing!

Among innumerable insects, I'll single out only the ant
between the border guard's left and right boots
blithely ignoring the questions "Where from?" and "Where to?"

Oh, to register in detail, at a glance, the chaos
prevailing on every continent!
Isn't that a privet on the far bank
smuggling its hundred-thousandth leaf aross the river?
And who but the octopus, with impudent long arms,
would disrupt the sacred bounds of territorial waters?

And how can we talk of order over-all
when the very placement of stars
leaves us doubting just what shines for whom?

Not to speak of the fog's reprehensible drifting!
And dust blowing all over the steppes
as if they hadn't been partitioned!
And the voices coasting on obliging airwaves,
that conspiratorial squeaking, those indecipherable mutters!

Only what is human can truly be foreign.
The rest is mixed vegetation, subversive moles, and wind.

Psalm

O, jakże są nieszczelne granice ludzkich państw!
Ile to chmur nad nimi bezkarnie przepływa,
ile piasków pustynnych przesypuje się z kraju do kraju,
ile górskich kamyków stacza się w cudze włości
w wyzywających podskokach!

Czy muszę tu wymieniać ptaka za ptakiem jak leci,
albo jak właśnie przysiada na opuszczonym szlabanie?
Niechby to nawet był wróbel – a już ma ogon ościenny,
choć dzióbek jeszcze tutejszy. W dodatku – aleź się wierci!

Z nieprzeliczonych owadów poprzestanę na mrówce,
która pomiędzy lewym a prawym butem strażnika
na pytanie: skąd dokąd – nie poczuwa się do odpowiedzi.

Och, zobaczyć dokładnie cały ten nieład naraz,
na wszystkich kontynentach!
Bo czy to nie liguster z przeciwnego brzegu
przemyca poprzez rzekę stutysięczny listek?
Bo kto, jeśli nie mątwa zuchwale długoramienna,
narusza świętą strefę wód terytorialnych?

Czy można w ogóle mówić o jakim takim porządku,
jeżeli nawet gwiazd nie da się porozsuwać,
żeby było wiadomo, która komu świeci?

I jeszcze to naganne rozpościeranie się mgły!
I pylenie się stepu na całej przestrzeni,
jak gdyby nie był wcale w pół przecięty!
I rozleganie się głosów na usłużnych falach powietrza:
przywoławczych pisków i znaczących bulgotów!

Tylko co ludzkie potrafi być prawdziwie obce.
Reszta to lasy mieszane, krecia robota i wiatr.

Wisława Szymborska, 1976
(trans. Clare Cavanagh and Stanisław Barańczak)

WISŁAWA SZYMBORSKA I love
this poem by Wisława Szymborska,
the Polish poet who won the
Nobel Prize for Literature in 1996.
Her profoundly humane, gently
humorous poetry is a true salve
for the soul in a technological 21st
century full of beeping pagers,
mobile phones, and incoming
message alerts.

Sugar Bread

My daily village errands, as the youngest member of the family, included getting fresh bread from the local bakery. The baker was a jolly, elderly man, with eyelashes and eyebrows white with flour. Each morning he used to hand me a warm loaf and ask me to send his best wishes to my grandmother. Aged five or six I could not resist chewing on the hot, crisp crust on the walk back home. Eventually I handed a half-eaten loaf to Józefa. She would look at it and smile, promising to have another word with the baker about his mice.

During breaks in play with my friend Janek next door, his mum fed us bread spread thick with butter and sugar. Janek only wanted slices from the middle of the loaf: those from the round ends, he said, were too small. The butter would melt into the bread, still warm from the baker, and I needed both hands to support the giant sugary slices.

I couldn't wait to have this forgotten delicacy again. I bought a freshly baked loaf from the village bakery. I smeared it with soft, yellow butter and plunged it into a pile of white sugar, pressing down firmly so as not to miss a single crystal. I hid with my fairy bread behind the kitchen door and took a first bite after 40 long years… it tasted as sweet as my memories. I was five years old again and I could hear Józefa warning me that I would spoil my appetite for dinner.

114

BREAD FOR THE HORSES

We were never allowed to throw out unwanted
bread in Poland. You could eat it, toast it, fry
it, soak it in milk, feed it to the birds on your
window sill or grow your own penicillin mould
on it, but you could NOT put it in the rubbish.
In the city my mother bought a quarter of a fresh
loaf each afternoon – enough for supper and
breakfast without guilt about wastage. The only
approved way to dispose of bread leftovers was
to collect them "for a horse" (*chleb dla konia*) by
leaving them in a separate bag next to the rubbish.
I imagined as a child that somewhere on the
outskirts of every town was a giant horse of Trojan
proportions, gratefully accepting stale bread from
the citizens. Today I notice that unwanted loaves
continue to be separated and left for collection.
Bread is still respected and every crumb recycled to
feed farm animals and birds.

First Communion

After weeks of negotiation between my devout great grandmother Julia and somewhat less religious parents it had been agreed that I would be allowed to take my first communion at the church in Jelenia Góra. I was relieved. The appeal of a white, lacy, tailor-made dress with a frill, which would gently fall over my lustrous white shoes, could only enhance my childish religious zeal and devotion. I would be a princess for one special day, and my family would look at me with misty eyes, astonished at my elegance and poise. When that special Sunday arrived, I felt like Snow White and floated down the aisle for God to admire my first long dress.

A massive feast followed, with every classic Polish dish: cured ham, baked chicken, veal cutlets with wild mushroom sauce, Russian Salad, biscuits, tarts, and jellies to follow. My favourite dessert, however, was my grandmother's angel wings (*faworki*) – sugar biscuits that she prepared that morning and dusted with shimmery icing sugar a few minutes before the guests arrived.

BELOW Beata, second row, far left, at her First Communion in the church in Jelenia Góra.

Angel Wings § FAWORKI

In medieval times ladies tied coloured ribbons to their knights' armour before they went into battle to wish them luck and remind them who would be waiting when they returned. *Faworki* are named for such "favours". Sometimes known as Angel Wings in English – or *chrust* (little sticks) in Polish – they are sweet crispy pastries in the shape of thin twisted ribbons, deep-fried, and sprinkled with icing sugar.

MAKES 30–40 PIECES

500 g (1 lb 2 oz) PLAIN (ALL-PURPOSE) FLOUR

5 EGG YOLKS

2 TEASPOONS SPIRITUS (SEE PAGE 32) OR WHITE VINEGAR

4 TABLESPOONS SOUR CREAM

2 TABLESPOONS ICING SUGAR

1 l (34 fl oz) VEGETABLE OIL FOR DEEP FRYING

Sift the flour onto a wooden board, make a hollow in the middle, and use your hands to mix in the egg yolks, spiritus, icing sugar, and sour cream to form a pastry dough. Knead the dough well until it is smooth.

Divide the dough into manageable chunks and, on a floured board, roll out each piece so it is about 2 mm (¼ in) thick. Cut the thin dough into strips about 3 cm (1 in) wide and 15 cm (6 in) long. Dust the pastry with a little extra flour if it is sticky to handle.

Cut a slit in the middle of each strip and thread one end through this hole to make a bow shape.

Heat the oil to 190°C (375°F) and deep fry the strips until they are golden but not brown.

Remove them carefully from the oil and allow to drain on kitchen paper. Sprinkle the *faworki* with icing sugar before serving.

Russian Salad § SAŁATKA JARZYNOWA

Russian Salad is a popular party dish, made with mayonnaise and often decorated – my grandmother put roses carved out of carrot peelings on top. The recipe also has a more humble life as a day-to-day snack, in bars and cafeterias, even at railway stations.

You can make this with your own fresh mayonnaise or one of the good-quality egg mayonnaises available by the jar.

SERVES 4 AS A STARTER

4 MEDIUM-SIZED POTATOES

5 CARROTS

1 PARSNIP

½ CELERIAC

2 DESSERT APPLES, PEELED

3 HARD-BOILED EGGS

2 SMALL PICKLED CUCUMBERS (SEE PICKLING RECIPE, PAGE 22)

1 LEEK (WHITE PART ONLY) OR WHITE ONION

1 TEASPOON ENGLISH MUSTARD

½ JAR EGG MAYONNAISE (c. 250 g (9 oz))

125g (4 ½ oz) COOKED GREEN PEAS

Wash the vegetables well, peeling and cutting if necessary. Boil the potatoes, carrots, parsnip, and celeriac and cook until they are just starting to soften (but avoid overcooking them as they will then be not so easy to slice and chop). Strain and allow to cool.

When cool, cut all the cooked vegetables into little cubes the same size – 6 mm (¼ in) is good – but you can choose your own size.

Also chop the apples, eggs, cucumbers, and leek or onion to the same size.

Mix all the ingredients together in a large bowl with the mustard, mayonnaise, and peas.

Season with salt and pepper. You can add more pickled cucumber if you would like a more piquant taste.

Serve with fresh bread.

Lidia's Roast Chicken § KURCZAK Z NADZIENIEM

This is my mother Lidia's special way to cook a chicken, roasting it with pâté-like stuffing.

SERVES 4

1 MEDIUM-SIZED FRESH CHICKEN (c. 2 kg (4 lb 7 oz))

2 EGGS

150 g (5 oz) WHITE BREADCRUMBS

50 g (2 oz) CHICKEN LIVERS, MINCED

1 BUNCH FLAT LEAF PARSLEY

50 g (2 oz) UNSALTED BUTTER

Preheat the oven to 180°C (350°F) and remove the neck and any giblets from inside the chicken.

Separate the eggs, mixing the egg yolks with the breadcrumbs and minced chicken livers. Chop the parsley finely then stir it through the mix.

Beat the egg whites until fluffy then fold them into the stuffing mix.

Fill the chicken cavity with the stuffing.

Rub the chicken with the butter and season with salt and pepper.

Bake for just 5 minutes to seal in the juices, then turn the oven down to 160°C (320°F) and cook for a further 70 minutes, or until the chicken is perfectly golden and the juices run clear when you insert a skewer into the thickest part of the meat. Carve the stuffing and serve in slices with the chicken.

Return of the Stork

Strawberry Fruit Pudding *§* KISIEL

Kisiel is another special party treat for kids, a very old-fashioned dessert that my grandmother's grandmother used to make for her. Invented before packet gelatine or jelly crystals were available, it was thickened with potato flour. This recipe is for strawberry *kisiel,* but works with other fresh summer fruit such as raspberries, or cherries with their stones removed.

SERVES 4

500 g (1 lb 2 oz) STRAWBERRIES

500 ml (17 fl oz) WATER

6 TABLESPOONS CASTER (SUPERFINE) SUGAR

8 TEASPOONS POTATO FLOUR

Wash, drain, and roughly chop the fruit, then place in a saucepan with the sugar and water. Cook for 5 minutes on a moderate heat or until soft.

Put the mixture through a sieve, pushing the fruit with the back of a spoon to extract all the juice. Pour the juice back into the saucepan.

Dissolve the potato flour in 100 ml (3 fl oz) of cold water and slowly mix into the fruit mixture, then bring to the boil, stirring constantly until it thickens into a smooth soft jelly.

Pour into dessert glass bowls that have been rinsed with warm water (to stop the hot liquid cracking the glass). The pudding can be eaten warm straight away, or served cold later. It is often topped with vanilla-sugared fresh cream or custard.

Return of the Stork

Summer in Poland

Last summer Simon and I returned to Poland for a grand tour. We set off on a long car journey together; our aim – to visit as many of Poland's old towns and cities as we could and get lost in the dreamy summer countryside. Never missing a restaurant, café, or patisserie, we ate ten times a day and drank far too many wines and spirits in local bars. It is a hard job researching a cookery book!

We weren't in a hurry, so we took my uncle's advice and avoided the busy east–west highways, where big trucks have been crossing the country for decades, wearing ruts in the road surface. Instead we discovered a near-empty network of minor byways that took us on a Snakes and Ladders course across the country. The nearest things to speed cameras were massive storks' nests, balanced precariously on utility poles. We drove through an idyllic land, with unfenced green farms adorned with hibiscus and sunflowers, the occasional farm worker asleep under a tree. We saw children abandon their bikes on the edge of a forest, back wheels still spinning. I so wanted to join them for a game of hide and seek.

No day was the same, as the landscape changed from sea to lake to forest to mountains. Loaded with history books and guides, we read aloud as we drove, entranced by local legends and history. We'd often pull over to chat to people, on the pretext of seeking directions. After a few more minutes of driving we would come to an abrupt halt once again to say hello to stern goats or horses patrolling the road. We drove and stopped, drove and stopped, forever changing our time of arrival at the next destination. As our fascination with Poland grew, Simon took thousands of photos. I watched him fall in love with the country of my childhood, and felt very proud to have been born here.

My first road trip

I remember the first time I went on a road trip without my parents: it was a school excursion to Wrocław zoo. The bus journey was about 100 kilometres (60 miles) each way – three hours along an old, German-built autobahn. The thump-thump rhythm of the bus as we bumped over each concrete slab soon sent me to sleep. Aged six, 100 kilometres was a magic number. For me it was a trans-global expedition and I did not believe anyone could possibly travel farther than this, though I knew we'd be safely back with our parents in time for the evening news.

Our families provided food for the day: hard-boiled eggs, rye bread with *smalec* (dripping), and a stoppered bottle of very strong, cold black tea with lots of sugar – the 1960s

equivalent of an energy drink. This was meant
to last us all day but we were so excited we
had finished our rations before the mountains
of Jelenia Góra had disappeared behind us.
Within a short distance the bus would come
to an abrupt stop for some child to throw up
their boiled eggs amongst the roadside bushes,
while the rest of us were glued to the window,
fascinated by such a medical emergency.
The thrill of travelling on our own without
parents in that barrel of aluminum with its
green vinyl seats was intoxicating.

Bacon Spread on Rye Bread § SMALEC

Smalec was once a poor man's food but it can be found today on the menu of many up-market Polish restaurants as a popular appetizer.

ENOUGH FOR 4

250 g (9 oz) STREAKY BACON (WITH PLENTY OF FAT ON THE RIND) OR SPECK

1 TABLESPOON WATER

1 ONION, CHOPPED

1 TEASPOON FRESH MARJORAM, CHOPPED

Chop the bacon into small cubes and place in a saucepan with the water on a low heat. Once the fat has melted and looks glass-like, throw in the chopped onion and fry until golden in colour. Add the marjoram and season to taste.

Scoop into a stone cup or earthenware ramekin. Stir as it cools so the little bits of bacon stay suspended and don't settle on the bottom.

Keep it in a cool place and serve on dark rye bread sprinkled with salt, or use for cooking – it adds wonderful extra flavour when refrying yesterday's *pierogi*.

Wrocław

Wrocław was my first university town. I arrived here by train as an 18-year-old student with a suitcase full of dreams, ambitions, and my grandmother's preserves. Now I could finally study medicine and keep the promise I made to Józefa. I was so keen to get started I arrived a week early by mistake, and had to stay with some surprised but welcoming relatives for the last few days of the long summer break, before the university finally opened. As it was, the tumultuous events of 1980s Poland resulted in my family's migration, and I ended up completing my medical degree eight years later in Australia.

Now driving into Wrocław after so long the first thing Simon was struck by was a huge grey cemetery along the road that leads into town. Hundreds and hundreds of headstones seemed to be marching on the city in the footsteps of fallen Russian soldiers, who had fought the Germans for control of the city in the last months of the Second World War. Today both Russian and German can be heard alongside Polish, English, and other languages in the many beer bars around Wrocław's main square. The new generation of European youth, partying together, is probably not too sure what that desperate conflict was all about.

BELOW CENTRE Wrocław Town Hall
FOLLOWING PAGES Town houses on Wrocław's main square.

WROCŁAW

The middle of summer in the middle of Poland... my midsummer dream, I thought, as we headed off into fields of wheat and cabbages, and forests of cherry trees. Sometimes we stopped at the roadside to buy fresh fruit from the local kids. They giggled with joy when we bought their fruit without bargaining, happily paying a couple of złoty (about a dollar) for a small punnet of freshly picked wild blueberries, raspberries, or redcurrants. Laughing, they waved us goodbye, hardly believing that a tourist had driven through their village. We devoured our fruit while driving, our lips and fingers permanently stained with blueberry and cherry juice.

I loved the earthy smell of the fruits and vegetables for sale in the market squares of many small Polish towns. Farmers came daily to sell their produce: there were unwashed carrots and beetroot, cabbages and onions. It was OK here to feel the potatoes, squeeze a parsnip for its vigour, or sniff a bunch of garlic for a quick high. The heady scents took me back to Julia's dark and mysterious cellar.

The market atmosphere makes transactions short and loud. Money is exchanged behind mountains of cucumbers and tomatoes, coins disappearing quickly into the berry-stained apron pockets of the sellers.

Summer in Poland

There was no need to label the produce "organic" – there was no other kind of farming here – and it was all truly seasonal. I asked an old man if he had any plums. It was July. He shook his head with contempt. "*Na drzewie!*" ("They're still on the tree!") Instead I bought two punnets of wild strawberries – and tried to hide my embarrassment from the customers waiting patiently behind me for their bunches of dill for pickling cucumbers. I resolved to come back in September to show the old man that I knew perfectly well when plums fell off the trees.

145

Plum-filled Potato Dumplings

KNEDLE ZE ŚLIWKAMI

In late summer, the plums were finally ripe and falling off the trees, turning the grass beneath into a purple carpet. Before they were converted into plum jam or plum butter (*powidła*), dried for Christmas, or made into compote, a grandmother with some time on her hands would make plum dumplings – a true treat for the children. The dumplings burst on the plate and release a sweet, ruby syrup that mixes deliciously with the accompanying custard or cream sauce. For the chance of a plum treat the village kids would visit everyone's grandmother for two brief weeks every summer and be on their best behaviour. During that magical time it was possible to eat plum dumplings for lunch every day – in different grandmothers' houses.

MAKES 10 LARGE DUMPLINGS (1–2 PER PERSON)

5 MEDIUM-SIZED UNWASHED POTATOES

300 g (11 oz) PLAIN (ALL-PURPOSE) FLOUR

1 EGG

10 ANGELINA, BLOOD, OR ANY LARGE RIPE PLUMS

110 g (4 oz) BUTTER

5 TABLESPOONS BREADCRUMBS (OR CRUSHED CORN FLAKES)

300 g (11 oz) CASTER (SUPERFINE) SUGAR

1 TEASPOON GROUND CINNAMON

FOR THE CREAM SAUCE

250 ml (8 fl oz) FRESH LIGHT OR SINGLE CREAM

4 TEASPOONS VANILLA SUGAR

½ TEASPOON CINNAMON

Peel the potatoes and boil in salted water until tender, then mash and allow to cool. My grandmother always used last season's crop of potatoes for this recipe as older ones are more starchy and less watery than the fresh.

Sieve the flour onto the mashed potato and mix in the egg by hand to form a dough mixture. Divide it into 5 cm- (2 in-) diameter balls. Roll these out into circles about 5 mm (¼ in) thick and 15 cm (6 in) across on a pre-floured wooden board. Each circle should be large enough to wrap around a plum.

Cut each plum in half, remove the stone, and put a teaspoon of sugar in the hollow in the middle. Place the 2 halves back together, then enclose in a pastry dough circle, pinching the pastry together and smoothing it so it is an even thickness all around the plum.

Drop the balls into fresh boiling water for about 5 minutes or until they float to the surface. Remove and drain.

Melt the butter in a saucepan and mix in the breadcrumbs, sugar, and cinnamon. Cook together for a few minutes.

Roll each ball in the breadcrumb mix until evenly coated.

To make the cream sauce, lightly whisk the ingredients together and serve alongside the dumplings.

Cucumber Season

July and August were the long-awaited summer months when everything would shut: schools, universities, theatres, and ministries. People came out of their winter cocoons and, like ancient Egyptians, looked up to the sky, praying to Ra for warm rays to brown their pale faces.

Summer was compulsory, clothes sleeveless, shoes swapped for sandals, *pierogi* filled with blueberries, and soup made from young beetroot shoots. We watched weather maps on TV with trepidation, hoping the cold front over the Azores would not reach us, freezing Western rather than Eastern Europe.

My grandmother Józefa called it cucumber season (*sezon ogórkowy*) – when the only thing to do was watch the cucumbers growing. We used to walk together slowly through the empty streets of Jelenia Góra. She would promise strawberry roulade that night if I stopped looking bored. When that didn't work she said if I cheered up we would make puppets from the husks of Julia's poppies and some old socks: "our own little theatre" she enthused, pulling my hand so I was forced into a joyful hop.

Cucumber Salad MIZERIA

Mizeria appears on every menu in Poland, a summer side dish of finely sliced cucumbers and sour cream. Different versions include freshly chopped chives or dill, and onion.

MAKES ENOUGH FOR 4

500 g (1 lb 2 oz) CUCUMBERS

125 ml (4 fl oz) SOUR CREAM

1 TABLESPOON DILL, CHOPPED

A PINCH OF CASTER (SUPERFINE) SUGAR

½ ONION, CHOPPED (OPTIONAL)

Wash the cucumbers and peel them. Using a grater with a wide slicing blade, slice the cucumber thinly.

Mix it with the sour cream and chopped dill. Sprinkle over the sugar, and season with salt and pepper and a little onion if desired.

Józefa's Cucumber Soup § ZUPA OGÓRKOWA

This popular Polish soup can be made from scratch as my grandmother did, making your own chicken stock prior to adding the vegetables, or you can use a good-quality, ready-made stock instead. It will save about an hour of cooking, if you do.

SERVES 4

FOR THE STOCK (BOUILLON)

2 CHICKEN WINGS

½ MEDIUM ONION

4 SPRIGS CURLY-LEAF PARSLEY

1 WHOLE CARROT

½ PARSNIP

2 TEASPOONS SALT

FOR THE SOUP

2 CARROTS

½ CELERIAC

1 PARSNIP

5 MEDIUM-SIZED POTATOES, WASHED, PEELED, AND CUT INTO 2–3 cm (1 in) CUBES

6 MEDIUM-SIZED BRINE-PICKLED (NOT VINEGAR-PICKLED) CUCUMBERS (SEE PAGE 22), FINELY GRATED

2 TABLESPOONS SOUR CREAM

1 BUNCH FRESH DILL, CHOPPED

Place all the ingredients for the stock in a saucepan and cover with about 2 litres (4 pints) of water. Bring to the boil and simmer for at least an hour. (You may want to scoop any unwanted chicken fat from the surface before the next stage.)

To make the soup, wash and peel the carrots, the celeriac, and the parsnip and cut them into 1 cm (½ in) cubes. Add these to the stock and simmer for a further 10 minutes.

Remove the chicken wings. Scoop out half a cup of soup and mix with the cream.

Add the cubed potatoes and simmer for 5–10 minutes until they have softened, then add the grated cucumber and the soup/cream mix. Simmer gently for a few more minutes. Season with salt and pepper.

Serve hot with plenty of fresh dill sprinkled on top.

Beetroot-shoot Soup § BOTWINKA

Beetroot, or "beets", is a highly nutritious vegetable, and not just the red root commonly eaten, but the fresh leaves and stalks as well. This recipe only works with young beetroot shoots – in Poland that means those picked in June or July – as by September the beetroot stalks are too fibrous.

SERVES 6

STALKS AND LEAVES OF 6 BEETROOTS

2 l (4 pints) MEAT STOCK OR BOUILLON (BEEF OR CHICKEN)

1 WHOLE BEETROOT ROOT

1 CLOVE GARLIC

1 TEASPOON SALT

1 TEASPOON DRY MARJORAM

1 TEASPOON LEMON JUICE

6 EGGS, HARD-BOILED

250 ml (8 fl oz) FRESH SINGLE POURING CREAM

Wash the beetroot leaves and stalks well then pat dry with a paper towel. Chop them into small pieces. The leaves will shrink when cooked, so you will need quite a few. Add the chopped beetroot stalks and leaves to the stock and simmer until soft, for about 15 minutes.

Grind a clove of garlic with a teaspoon of salt on a wooden board, then add to the soup with a teaspoon of dry marjoram and a teaspoon of lemon juice.

Wash, peel, and score the beetroot bulb with grooves. Add to the soup to bring out a wonderful colour. Simmer for a further 10 minutes.

Cut the hard-boiled eggs into halves or quarters, then season with salt and pepper.

Leaving the whole beetroot in the pot, ladle the soup into individual bowls and place a good splash of fresh cream in each. Serve hot and garnish with the hard-boiled eggs.

Summer in Poland

Poznań

On a bright July day the old town of Poznań was full of young people. The universities and schools had finally released their inmates to soak up some sun and ventilate their lungs from the dust of old libraries. And here they were, young Poles everywhere, occupying coffee shops, fountain steps, lawns, and benches. I remember that special feeling of elation during the first days of the long school holidays, when everything seemed possible. The pale rays of sun made daring plans pile up in my head. This summer would bring a life-changing adventure, a surprise discovery, a passionate first romance.

BELOW RIGHT Postcard of Chwaliszewski Bridge, Poznań, c1910.

CZERWONE
GITARY

To właśnie my

XL 0350
HI-FI

Summer in Poland

LEFT *Czerwone Gitary* album cover. On Sunday afternoons Józefa and I listened to *Koncert Życzeń* on the radio. I always hoped for a song by my favourite band *Czerwone Gitary* so I could dance and perform, wooden spoon in hand, in front of our large yellow radio. More often it was Józefa's favourite bass baritone Bernard Ładysz singing Moniuszko's "Clock Aria". OPPOSITE, LEFT Poznań's magnificent Renaissance Town Hall. OPPOSITE, FAR RIGHT Poznań's Opera House.

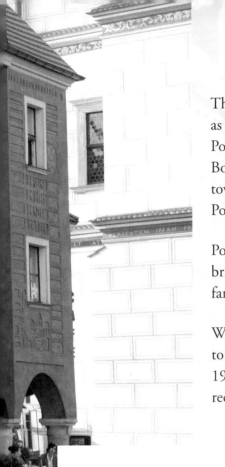

The city of Poznań was founded over 1000 years ago on an island, known as the Ostrów Tumski, surrounded by two branches of the Warta River. Poland's first king, Mieszko I, built his castle here, and he and his son Bolesław the Brave lie in tombs in the Golden Chapel inside Poznań's six-towered cathedral. Mieszko was the prince who accepted Christianity into Poland and his baptism in 966 marked the beginning of the Polish state.

Poznań soon outgrew the tiny island and the main Market Square, with its brightly painted merchant houses and an Italian-designed town hall now famous for its Renaissance loggias, was built to the west of the river.

We squeezed past chatting couples on the steps of Poznań's opera house to get a look at this grand building. It was named after Poland's famous 19th-century composer Stanisław Moniuszko whose "Clock Aria" was most requested on Poland's radio song dedication programme *Koncert Życzeń*.

163

The Library and Arboretum at Kórnik Castle

It is hard to imagine a more romantic setting for a library than the 14th-century castle at Kórnik. The thick walls, ancient park, and wide moat defend century-old texts from outside noise and the approaching army of e-books. Among the 400,000 volumes are stored many treasures of Polish literature and science including Copernicus' most famous book *De revolutionibus orbium coelestium* (On the Revolutions of the Celestial Spheres; *O obrotach ciał niebieskich*). There are also works by the Renaissance poet Jan Kochanowski, whose limericks I learned at school. The limerick on the loss of good health ought to be written on the waiting-room walls of every doctor.

Magnificent trees and flowering shrubs await visitors to Kórnik's arboretum, their beauty and exuberance matched by the flamboyant Latin names scribbled on small metal labels. *Aesculus hippocastanum* stands here, so... show some respect and learn botanics, the sign seemed to be saying, you *Ignoramus Magnificus*. Like a psychedelic dream, purples, pinks, and reds of lilac and azalea blossoms swirled together, their fragrances mixed in an exquisite perfume no technology could reproduce. There was no sky left in this park, it had been replaced by a high ceiling of leaves in all shades of green, supported by columns of grooved and mossy bark. I could have spent the whole summer here, hugging trees and counting magnolia petals, but I had the rest of Poland to explore, before returning to Australia, land of olive eucalypts and golden wattles.

ON HEALTH
(*Na zdrowie*)

Oh good health,
No one knows
How fine you taste,
Until you fail...

Szlachetne zdrowie,
Nikt się nie dowie,
Jako smakujesz,
Aż się zepsujesz...

Jan Kochanowski, 1576

ABOVE Page from the first edition of *De revolutionibus orbium coelestium* by Copernicus. OPPOSITE Medioval xylograph of a biblical scene from the collection at Kórnik Library.

Summer in Poland

Wielkopolska

One sunny Sunday morning we drove through the countryside of Wielkopolska. We headed roughly north, in the general direction of the coast, taking whatever obscure route took our fancy. We were soon alone on a road that wound through wide golden wheatfields and green apple orchards, with the shadows of clouds and birds drowning in sky blue lakes. The small villages seemed sleepy, only church doors wide open, hungry for Sunday worshippers. My English husband who had spent childhood holidays in Provence declared the landscape as beautiful as the south of France. Of course I argued it was more peaceful, picturesque, and unspoiled, while crushing a fragrant sprig of lavender in my hand. As we drove we saw windmills turning on the horizon – poignant symbols of this part of Poland and its long agricultural history. "Wielkopolska is Poland's pantry", my high-school geography book said. "The birthplace of the Polish nation" my history book added. We ditched our travel schedule yet again and headed for the windmills, while I tried to impress Simon by reciting a complete list of Polish kings.

Trout Smoked with Apple Wood § PSTRĄG WĘDZONY

My father's friend Jurek makes a tasty smoked trout in his homemade smoker. He uses a variety of wood but his favourite is dried apple tree branches that he gathers from his own orchard. Trout-smoking day is a great excuse for a party. While Jurek marinates the fish, hangs it on wet string, and stokes his smoker, we all sit on his shady verandah eating, drinking, and chatting while waiting for the trout to cure. "One more hour" Jurek finally announces at the end of a long afternoon, to which we all respond by opening more wine, frying more *pierogi,* and eating more Russian Salad. One has to know how to be patient! Finally the first fish is ready to be tested – pink and soft, with a delicate flavour and a hint of apples.

A smoker is simply a device to direct smoke around the fish. The flesh is cured by the warm smoke and infused with the flavour of the wood. (You can use the hardwood from any fruit tree.) The only rule for backyard inventors when designing your own smoker is that it should be made of wood and string, but no metal (which would get hot and cook the fish directly). Jurek smokes 20 fish at a time, but you can scale this down if you want to experiment and don't feel the need to share with all your family and friends.

FOR 20 TROUT

500 g (1 lb 2 oz) GRANULATED SUGAR

1 kg (2 lb 3 oz) SALT

10 l (2 ½ GALLONS) WATER

20 TROUT

Heat the water, add the sugar and salt, and stir until dissolved. Allow to cool.

Clean, scale, and gut the trout. Thread a length of string about 30 cm (1 ft) long through the head of each fish and tie to form a loop. Soak all the fish (and the string – so it doesn't burn in the smoker) in the salt and sugar solution for at least 2 hours. The flesh should then start to look shiny.

Build a fire from apple-wood branches and add some damp leaves or sawdust to make it smoky. Hickory and mesquite wood are also good to use. The idea is to keep a pile of smouldering wood, rather than flaming logs, below the fish. Suspend the threaded fish above the smouldering fire from a piece of wood, arranged so the smoke rises up past the fish. Leave for 4–5 hours, adding more wood chips every half hour or so to keep the fire smoking.

Let the fish settle for an hour or so before eating. The flesh should be pink and soft. Smoked trout with bread and salad makes a sumptuous summer meal.

Summer in Poland

Apple Pancakes § PLACKI Z JABŁKAMI

These are small, sweet pancakes served for breakfast or afternoon tea. My grandmother placed whole apple slices on the batter while it was still sizzling in the pan.

MAKES 8 PANCAKES

2 EGGS

350 ml (12 fl oz) MILK

2 TABLESPOONS CASTER (SUPERFINE) SUGAR

300 g (11 oz) SELF-RAISING FLOUR

4 SMALL EATING APPLES

50 g (2 oz) UNSALTED BUTTER FOR FRYING

ICING (POWDERED) SUGAR FOR DECORATION

Whisk the eggs, milk, and sugar together, then fold in the flour. (These pancakes are like pikelets and need to be thick and fluffy so it is best not to use an electric mixer.) Add a pinch of salt, cover, and put aside for 30 minutes.

Peel the apples, cut into halves, de-core, and slice thinly.

Melt a knob of butter in a hot frying pan and add a dollop of the batter mix to form a pancake. Lay 1 or 2 slices of apple on top of the batter then fry for a couple of minutes. Turn over and cook the other side.

Sprinkle with icing (powdered) sugar and serve hot.

Baltic Sea

ABOVE LEFT Beata's mother Lidia. ABOVE RIGHT Beata aged two.

We spent the whole day exploring the vast dunes (*wydmy*) near the seaside town of Łeba. To reach them we took a slow boat ride along Lake Łebsko, then walked through an ancient forest of pines that whispered in the wind. (The noise of wind in trees is so common in highly wooded Poland there is even a word, *szumi* – pronounced "shoomy" – to describe this very soothing sound.) Finally we reached the mountainous, desert-like dunes by the beach. Waves of white sand fused with white clouds in the distance, dreamy and hypnotic. Other tourists on the horizon looked small and insignificant, tiny black dots moving across white swirling sand that covered their footprints the instant they lifted their feet. The wind was bracing even in July. It whipped the grey sea into a froth of snowy foam, seemingly suspended mid-air, frozen against the pale blue sky.

Kolonie

During the summer holidays, like all Polish schoolchildren, I was sent away on summer camp – *kolonie*. We were the mountain kids so we were always bussed off to the sea for our summer break. I was sure that somewhere in the middle of Poland we would cross paths with all the coastal children in another bus on their journey to the mountains. We sang all the way: Russian war songs, communist marching songs, scout and student songs, songs we heard on TV. Some of the lyrics were printed on the back of my grandmother's newspaper *Girlfriend* (*Przyjaciółka*). For years I dutifully cut out the words and music and pasted them into scrapbooks – and I can still sing them today (ready for a song festival for 1960s school children?). Some of the drivers joined in, others gritted their teeth as we sang such contemporary classics as "Hurry up Driver, There's Half a Litre of Vodka Waiting in the Garage" (*Panie szofer gazu!*).

Whoever spotted the sea first was an instant hero. After hearing the shout "*Morze!*" ("Sea!") a busload of unrestrained children would rush to the front, crowding the driver and staring out at the magical strip of grey on the horizon. We were mesmerized by the limitless horizon of the sea, after spending months hemmed in by the mountains. Once at our destination, we were encouraged to take deep breaths to inhale the iodine in the air, which was supposed to have magical powers and guard us from infections. We were unloaded into an empty school building set up with camp beds, and fed a supper of fish paste on rye bread with yet more sweet black tea brewed in large enamel pots.

A three-week trip without parents, when only seven years old, was both scary and thrilling. We would write home every day, exaggerating the strict discipline and bad food, not mentioning the fun and excitement we were actually having. We received parcels of sweets, including barley sugar (*landrynki*), fudge (*krówki*), and chocolate as rewards for our courage. The more teary the letter, the bigger the parcel.

None of us knew how to swim, as we stood knee-deep in the Baltic, teeth chattering in the strong wind. We were made to hold hands in case

FOLLOWING PAGES Every trip
to the Baltic coast included a
visit to one of the largest
medieval fortresses in Europe –
Malbork Castle – a stronghold of
the Teutonic Knights.

someone slipped under the water, the teachers anxiously counting us back
onshore. I don't know how we could have gone missing when we were all
welded together by a frozen handshake. I laugh at the memory when I
watch our children swim like dolphins in the Australian surf today. Back
then we spent most of our time out of the water, scouring the beaches.
We knew there was treasure to be found. Maybe that golden nugget on
the sand would turn out to be precious amber and not just an exploding
bubble of seaweed.

Fortress on the Beach

As well as state-sponsored summer camps just for kids, in communist times employers provided holidays (*wczasy*) for the whole family – each year the same huts with the same fellow workers. Every day we went off to the beach, through the pines and over the dunes, and claimed our patch of sand with a windbreak (*parawan*) to guard against the ferocious onshore winds – and other holiday makers. Made from a long strip of fabric held in place with pointed wooden poles planted in the sand, the width and pattern of your *parawan* was a reflection of your social standing in the new beach community. It was a great thrill to lie still and wait for the wind to throw the entire contraption on top of the family, much to the frustration of the adults. Only then would the boredom of lying on the cold sand end for a moment while we rebuilt our fortress.

At lunchtime we took it in turns to stay behind and guard the *parawan* while the others ate a hot lunch back in the resort canteen. The appointed guard would be given a bread roll to chew on, saved from breakfast, while the rest of us rushed off, hoping for *pierogi* or *kluski śląskie*.

Polish beaches were provided with wicker basket seats (*kosze*) that early birds could reserve as a base for their family. In the evening when the adults had finally gone we children loved to grab the *kosze* for ourselves. We played hide and seek, or built rival camps behind the fallen basket seats, defending them to the last sandy bullet as the wet sand turned orange, and the sun sank somewhere over the horizon, far beyond Sweden.

Today many of the old communist resorts have been turned into beauty spas and clinics, advertising laser and botox treatments, and mantra and tantra for breakfast. I was thrilled to see families still camping among the trees.

ABOVE At the Baltic Sea with family and other holidaymakers. Left to right, Beata's father Grzegorz, Beata aged two, and her mother Lidia. RIGHT Waffles (*rurki z kremem*) are still for sale on the beach today. I lined up behind a crowd of school children as an old woman in a little stall slowly hand-filled the tubes with whipped cream. I impatiently awaited my turn, counting my place in the queue, but kept quiet in case anyone noticed my age.

184

GRZEGORZ' PAN-FRIED FLOUNDER

The resort breakfast was always *zupa mleczna* – hot milk with anything that could float, i.e. barley, rice, or noodles. The pungent smell of burnt milk woke up the camp better than any rooster.

Most holiday-makers took their milk soup without a word of complaint, frowning at the spoiled, post-war kids who ritually ran crying from the breakfast tables. Fortunately, my father Grzegorz had different ideas for breakfast. Most mornings he'd get up early, walk to the wharf, and befriend a local fisherman. He would cadge a fish off him, then come back with the freshest flathead or flounder. After gutting and washing the fish he salted it well on both sides and let it cure for an hour. Then he dusted it in plain flour (shaking off any excess) and fried it in a mixture of butter and oil in a very hot pan (about four minutes each side depending on the thickness of the fish). Served on fresh bread this is an irresistible outdoor breakfast and I have never tasted such delicious fish, despite visits to some very up-market seafood restaurants around the world since.

Herring in Sour Cream § ŚLEDZIE W ŚMIETANIE

This is a great appetiser especially when served with a cold shot of vodka. "Herring likes to swim", as the old Polish saying goes!

MAKES ENOUGH FOR 4

2 PICKLED HERRING FILLETS
c. 300 g (11 oz)

200 g (7 oz) SOUR CREAM

1 SMALL ONION

SMALL BUNCH FRESH DILL

FRESHLY GROUND BLACK PEPPER

Rinse the herring in cold water to remove excess salt and pat dry with paper towel. Slice it into 1 cm (½ in) squares.

Finely chop the onion and fresh dill and mix together with the fish. Add the sour cream and some pepper to taste.

Leave in the fridge for an hour for the flavours to develop.

Serve on thick slices of black bread – either rye or pumpernickel.

Summer in Poland

Gdańsk

The sky-high clock tower of the town hall governs the city, in charge of passing hours. Whether you like it or not, it's 12 o'clock again, as proclaimed by its loud bells. Back in Gdańsk after so long I'm thrilled to see Neptune's fountain once more. I have many old photographs of myself taken in front of it – a slightly older girl each year, from pony-tailed, laughing toddler to timid teenager, refusing to look at the camera. However, Neptune remains the same in all those photos, ignoring the instructions of passing time from the clock tower above. Strong and muscular, he is un-intimidated by a cloud of pigeons and forever ready to throw his triton.

When I came to Gdańsk as a child during summer holidays this was the place to buy all my souvenirs: a yearly supply of shell necklaces, ships in bottles, and perhaps an invaluable glass paperweight with sparkling snowflakes inside. All these treasures would clutter my bookshelves, the paperweight occasionally shaken to waken the mermaid inside.

As Simon and I walked through Gdańsk we saw red-and-white Solidarity banners everywhere – a reminder about where the end of the Cold War had begun. It was thanks to the brave men and women of the Gdańsk shipyards that migrants like me can return to enjoy the new democracy of a free Polish state. We visited the austere church of St Brigida, where Solidarity members once met in secret. We strolled along the restored Long Market, admiring the ornamented house facades, and gazed at the windows in Mariacka Street, full of dazzling amber jewelry. Then we entered impressive St Mary's Cathedral, the largest brick church in all of

Summer in Poland

GDAŃSK

TOP LEFT Cover by Andrzej Janicki and Filip Myszkowski of *Solidarność – 25 lat: Nadzieja zwykłych ludzi (Solidarity – 25 Years: Ordinary People Hope)* by Maciej Jasiński

Europe. Inside, young couples wandered hand in hand, stopping to kiss in front of the Madonna, perhaps making betrothal plans for their future.

Early on Saturday morning the Gdańsk markets were just setting up. It was a true growers' market with fresh fruit shining with the morning dew (rather than wax). A woman unpacked tiny wild strawberries for sale in recycled yoghurt containers, while an old man carefully piled his homegrown apples into a green pyramid. The big garden strawberries on sale were so ripe you could smell them from right across the square. They stained their wicker punnets with juice as red as the bricks of Gdańsk's inner city walls. I remember when in the communist era foreign goods were scarce and expensive in Poland. Now it was food marked "local" – *krajowe* – that was at a premium, more expensive than imported produce from other EC countries.

195

Three-day Strawberry Jam   KONFITURY TRUSKAWKOWE

This jam is very simple to make, even if it takes three days! It is equally good made from raspberries, blackberries, or gooseberries and can be stored for up to two years. Apart from spreading on bread, one or two teaspoons make a fruity sweetener spooned into a cup of hot tea, just as my violin teacher used to do.

MAKES APPROX 1.5 KG (3 LB 4 OZ) JAM

1 kg (2 lb 3 oz) STRAWBERRIES

1 kg (2 lb 3 oz) CASTER (SUPERFINE) SUGAR

Put the summer berries in a heavy-bottomed pan with the sugar and heat for 20 minutes until the sugar has melted and the fruit starts to soften. Shake the pan rather than stir it so that the fruit remains intact. Allow to cool, then cover and leave for 24 hours at room temperature.

The next day scoop off any foam that has formed on top. Heat as before and simmer gently for 20 minutes, then cover and leave for another 24 hours.

Repeat the process one more time but while the jam is still hot, pour it into sterilized jars and seal firmly.

To seal the lids, fill each jar right to the top with *konfitury*. Screw the lid on very tightly, and invert it. The heat of the jam now expands the metal lid.

After a minute try screwing the lid on another half turn while the jar is still upside down (you may need an oven glove). Then turn the jars the right way up; when the lids cool they contract to form tight seals.

Or you can fill the jars to leave a 2 cm (1 in) gap below the rims. Screw the lids on firmly. Place a tea towel or large clean dishcloth in the bottom of a big saucepan and stand the filled jars on it so they do not rattle when the water boils. Fill the pan with water to about halfway up the glass jars. With the lid on the pan, bring to the boil: the steam created in the pan expands the jar lids. After 5 minutes remove the jars and immediately tighten the lids further before allowing them to cool and form tight seals.

Strawberry Roulade § ROLADA Z TRUSKAWKAMI

The key to this simple but delicious recipe is to make a cake that is light and fluffy and flexible enough to roll up, like a Swiss roll.

ENOUGH FOR 6

110 g (4 oz) SELF-RAISING FLOUR

3 EGGS, LIGHTLY BEATEN

110 g (4 oz) CASTER (SUPERFINE) SUGAR

500 ml (17 fl oz) FRESH PURE OR WHIPPING CREAM

250 g (9 oz) STRAWBERRIES

ICING (POWDERED) SUGAR, FOR DUSTING

Preheat the oven to 160–180°C (320–350°F).

Beat the sugar and eggs until almost white, then fold in the flour.

Pour the mix into a shallow Swiss-roll tin (30 x 25 x 2 cm (12 x 10 x 1 in)) lined with baking paper (don't grease it) and cook in the oven for 12 minutes.

Remove, turn out onto a clean tea towel, and allow to cool.

Carefully peel off the baking paper. Slowly roll up the cake and the cloth together – the cloth helps to keep it in shape.

Stir a tablespoon of sugar into the cream and whip until thick.

Unroll the cake and remove the cloth.

Use a spatula to spread the cream over the cake. Slice some fresh strawberries and scatter them on top of the cream before carefully rolling up the cake again.

Decorate with more strawberries on the top and dust with icing (powdered) sugar. Slice thickly and serve with a cup of coffee or tea.

Misia's Strawberry Meringue

℘ CIASTO TRUSKAWKOWE

This summer dessert made with fresh strawberries is a favourite of little Misia, my Aunt Sabina's granddaughter. It is a fruit pastry cake with meringue and has a crumbly, biscuity base.

SERVES 4–6

1 kg (2 lb 3 oz) FRESH STRAWBERRIES

750 g (1 lb 10 oz) PLAIN FLOUR

200 g (7 oz) CASTER (SUPERFINE) SUGAR

250 g (9 oz) UNSALTED BUTTER

2 TEASPOONS BAKING POWDER

5 EGG YOLKS

6 EGG WHITES

8 TEASPOONS ICING (POWDERED) SUGAR

Wash, hull, and slice the fresh strawberries. Preheat the oven to 150°C (300°F) – do not use the fan setting for your oven.

Mix the flour, caster (superfine) sugar, butter, baking powder, and egg yolks together in a bowl. Use your hands to knead the ingredients into a pastry. Shape the dough into a couple of cylinders, about the size of Swiss rolls, wrap in plastic food wrap, and put in the freezer for a couple of hours.

Grease a large baking tray (33 x 23 x 5 cm (13 x 9 x 2 in)) with butter. When the pastry is hard enough, grate it onto the tray using a "number 1" grater – the largest "hole" on your grater. Flatten the crumbly pastry base a little by pressing down on it with the back of a spoon.

Beat the egg whites with a pinch of salt to form soft peaks. Slowly fold in the icing (powdered) sugar a teaspoon at a time. Now beat the egg whites until stiff.

Spread a couple of tablespoons of the meringue mix over the pastry base. Place sliced strawberries all over, then spoon on the rest of meringue mixture. Bake for about 50 minutes. The meringue browns lightly as it slowly cooks, but if it starts to burn, cover with a large sheet of baking paper.

Allow to cool before serving in generous squares.

Sopot

While on holiday on the Baltic coast my parents would take me on a short railway ride to Sopot, a seaside resort on the outskirts of Gdańsk. We walked out along the pier (*Molo*) and watched suntanned and elegantly dressed men and women strolling up and down a wooden platform that ventured daringly into the capricious Baltic swell. In the 1960s Sopot was like the French riviera, with international singers and film stars to be spotted on the pier. This was *the* place to show off your latest dress in a large bold print, flared trousers, teased hairdos, and giant cat-eye sunglasses. When the afternoon winds freshened, waves splashed up unexpectedly through the wooden planks stopping the fashion show abruptly. The salty shower melted the hairdos and tresses in an instant, forcing clothes to cling to voluptuous breasts and hips, and making men and children alike squeal with excitement.

Sopot Song Festival

As a child I couldn't wait for the beginning of the Sopot International Festival of Song. It was the only time I was allowed to stay up and watch TV past my normal bedtime. I would sit on Józefa's bed staring at the small, rounded, black-and-white screen, with a resolution worse than any

SOPOT

Summer in Poland

pre-war photo of my great-grandparents. The Festival took place in Sopot's open-air theatre, the Opera Leśna, with Lucjan Kydryński announcing international stars from communist-friendly countries such as East Germany, Romania, Cuba, Czechoslovakia, and of course the USSR.

On hot August nights, with a backing track of crickets and the summer fragrance of *maciejka* flowers from my grandmother's garden, the TV coverage of the Sopot Festival became my childhood window on the world, only sometimes obscured by large moths also attracted to the glitter of the event. Józefa watched with me; I sang along with all the songs and we both fantasized about travelling to the distant countries where the singers came from. Of course, my great-grandmother Julia had no time for such 20th-century trash culture. She would read Tolstoy late into the night, ignoring the TV and the world outside, occasionally glancing at her daughter and great-granddaughter with barely concealed contempt.

In the morning I would compete with my friend Bożena to see who had stayed up the latest. The dazzling festival gowns we had seen would become blueprints for the summer fashions. It would only take a few days for someone in the village to make a gown like Conchita Bautista's from Cuba, using tassles removed from an old German curtain.

BELOW Beata, aged three, with her mother Lidia and a friend.

You will come back here

"You will come back here" is a touching message to all Poles abroad that one day they will return to their homeland. Not long ago, when the children were finally asleep one night, I found a youTube video of Irena Santor performing this ballad. There I was in Sydney "far beyond seven mountains and seven rivers", suddenly choking back the tears, dreaming of returning to the banks of the Vistula River, the *"nadwiślański brzeg"*.

You will come back here

When you end up on a foreign shore
Sad to learn life's bitter truths
You start to miss where your family belong,
Then you'll come back here – where home is.

You'll come back here to Vistula's shores
Over seven mountains and rivers
Where heather and wild roses shine in the sun
And birches cast shadows on the sands of
  Mazovia.

You'll come back here, where willows line the
  fields,
Where white clouds flock like birds across the
  sky,
You'll come back to find your way and your stars
To hear again how the forests sing in spring.

Powrócisz tu

Gdy los cię rzuci gdzieś w daleki świat,
Gdy zgubisz szczęście swe i poznasz życia
  smak,
Zatęsknisz do rodzinnych stron
I wrócisz tu, wrócisz, gdzie twój dom.

Powrócisz tu, gdzie nadwiślański brzeg,
Powrócisz tu zza siedmiu gór i rzek,
Powrócisz tu, gdzie płonie słońcem wrzos i
  głóg,
Gdzie cienie brzóz, piach mazowieckich dróg.

Powrócisz tu, gdzie wierzby pośród pól,
Powrócisz tu, gdzie klucze białych chmur,
Powrócisz tu, by szukać swoich dróg i gwiazd,
Powrócisz tu! By słuchać znów, jak wiosną
  śpiewa las,

Lyrics by Janusz Kondratowicz, 1965
Music by Piotr Figiel

Irena Santor

Toruń

It was my childhood dream to study in Toruń, a university town on the banks of the Vistula River. Here was Copernicus' birthplace but more importantly the birthplace of thousands of ginger biscuits – *pierniki*. Eating chocolate biscuits obviously makes one clever, astronomically clever. Toruń is a fairytale town, with pretty houses and churches built, I believe, from gingerbread, hence the cinnamon and clover fragrance in the narrow cobblestoned streets. The statue of Copernicus stands in the old city centre, orbited by young students gravitating towards each other as evening falls and the earth turns away from the almighty sun.

We entered a shop that had dozens of variations of *pierniki*, all warm and freshly baked, stacked on shelves right up to the ceiling. I pointed to some shiny, round, milk-chocolate ones and ordered ten. The polite assistant asked if I wanted any more. Unsure of just how many you were meant to order, I chose another ten, this time coated with white chocolate. Anything else? Er, maybe the marzipan ones, please, filled with cherries? I just couldn't stop and left Toruń with piles of *pierniki* filling the back seat of the car. We had to eat them quickly if we were to see out of the back window. The car smelt of ginger and chocolate for the rest of our trip.

OPPOSITE ABOVE Reproduction of an image of medieval Toruń on linen. BELOW Portrait of Nicolaus Copernicus, artist unknown, 16th century.

FAFIK AND PROFESSOR FILUTEK

Professor Filutek and his dog Fafik appeared for years on the back of the newspaper *Przekrój*. Their creator, the Polish cartoonist Zbigniew Lengren, was born in Toruń in 1919. His cartoons ensured both children and adults read the newspaper. In the centre of the Old Town in Toruń we noticed that the absent-minded Professor had forgotten his umbrella again: it had been left leaning against a lamppost. Fafik stood by faithfully, his bronze head rubbed to a shine by hundreds of children who had patted and stroked this famous dog.

FLUTER

ZBIGNIEW LENGREN

Spiced Gingerbread Biscuits § PIERNIKI

According to legend the most famous *pierniki*, *Katarzynki*, were invented by accident. A Toruń baker had a daughter called Katarzyna (Katherine). One day he fell sick and asked his daughter to run the bakery on her own. She was anxious to help but when baking the *pierniki* she set the lumps of dough too close together. When she took them out of the oven the *pierniki* had fused together into the shape now known as *Katarzynki*. The legend goes that the people of Toruń bought Katarzyna's mis-shapen *pierniki* to reward her love and devotion for her sick father. *Katarzynki* are still popular today.

This recipe makes a light, spicy, biscuit-like gingerbread, perfect for cutting out. In Toruń you can buy gingerbread shaped liked the moon and the stars, even a *pierniki* portrait of Copernicus.

MAKES 12–15 MEDIUM-SIZED BISCUITS

600 g (1 lb 5 oz) PLAIN (ALL-PURPOSE) RYE FLOUR

½ TEASPOON GROUND CINNAMON

½ TEASPOON FRESHLY GROUND NUTMEG

½ TEASPOON GROUND CLOVES

½ TEASPOON ALL SPICE

350 g (12 oz) HONEY

4 EGGS

225 g (8 oz) CASTER (SUPERFINE) SUGAR

1 TEASPOON BAKING SODA

FOR THE GLAZE (OPTIONAL)

200 g (7 oz) ICING (POWDERED) SUGAR

1 TABLESPOON WATER

2 DROPS ALMOND ESSENCE

Preheat the oven to 180°C (350°F).

Sift the flour with the spices. Heat the honey until just boiling, then allow to cool to lukewarm.

Beat the eggs with the sugar until thick.

Dissolve the baking soda in a little water and add to the egg mixture, along with the honey, flour, and spices.

Blend well into a dough and roll out onto a lightly floured board to a thickness of about 5 mm (¼ in). Use a pastry cutter or knife to cut the dough into circles and stars, or whatever shape or pattern you might design.

Bake on a baking sheet lined with baking paper for about 10–15 minutes or until the *pierniki* are just turning brown. Carefully lift them with a spatula and allow to cool on a wire rack.

For the glazing, add the water slowly to the sugar and mix to a smooth paste with a couple of drops of almond essence. Spread over the *pierniki* with a palette knife or dip the biscuits into the icing and leave to set.

Elizabeth's Honeycake with Plum Jam

§ MIODOWNIK Z POWIDŁAMI

My Aunt Elizabeth makes this deliciously dark and chewy chocolate honeycake with layers of tangy plum jam. It takes a long time to make, but lasts for months in the fridge, tasting better the older it gets.

The jam used for the filling is a thick plum *powidła* or "plum butter" – a very popular concentrated jam. You can buy plum *powidła* in delis, or you could use another tangy filling such as marmalade.

MAKES 3 MEDIUM-SIZED CAKES

FOR THE CAKE

750 g (1 lb 10 oz) CASTER (SUPERFINE) SUGAR

2 TABLESPOONS WATER

250 g (9 oz) UNSALTED BUTTER

500 g (1 lb 2 oz) HONEY

3 TABLESPOONS ALLSPICE (POWDERED GINGER, CINNAMON AND CLOVES)

120 ml (4 fl oz) FULL CREAM MILK

3 TABLESPOONS BICARBONATE OF SODA

3 EGGS, BEATEN

1 kg (2 lb 3 oz) PLAIN (ALL-PURPOSE) FLOUR

FOR THE FILLING AND ICING

400 g (14 oz) PLUM BUTTER (*POWIDŁA*) OR ORANGE MARMALADE

500 g (1 lb 2 oz) COOKING CHOCOLATE

50 g (2 oz) UNSALTED BUTTER

First make the caramel. Put 3 tablespoons of the sugar in a saucepan with 2 tablespoons of water. Stir on a low heat to make a smooth brown caramel. Chop the butter into chunks and stir in. Now add the remaining sugar and the honey. Add the allspice and stir until the butter and sugar have blended in fully, then leave to cool to room temperature.

Stir in the milk and the bicarbonate of soda, along with the beaten eggs. Slowly work in the flour, little by little.

Preheat the oven to 200°C (400°F).

Divide the cake mix into 3 rectangular non-stick loaf tins, 21 x 11 x 6 cm (8½ x 4½ x 2½ in). The mix should be about 3 cm (1 in) deep in each. Bake for 10 minutes, then turn down the temperature to 180°C (350°F) and cook for another 50 minutes. The cakes will grow to nearly twice their size.

Remove from the oven and leave the cakes to cool in their tins. Once cool, turn them out, wrap in plastic food wrap, and leave in the fridge overnight.

Next day slice each cake horizontally into 4 or 5 slices about 1 cm (½ in) thick. The cake should be quite firm and easy to cut with a long sharp knife. Spread the jam generously on each layer before putting the cake back together. Now spread more jam on the top and sides. Leave to set while you make the icing.

Melt the cooking chocolate in a *bain marie* or double boiler. Add the butter and stir until smooth. Using a pallette knife coat the cake with the icing then return it to the fridge to set.

Serve in thin slices with a cup of coffee or tea.

Warszawa

It is hard to visit Warsaw (Warszawa in Polish) and not to think about its destruction more than half a century ago. The city ceased to exist at the end of the Second World War, buried under tons of gravel and smouldering ashes. Warsaw, the 20th-century Pompeii, was obliterated by Nazi bombs, which ultimately proved useless against the Polish spirit of survival.

Since the War the city has been painstakingly rebuilt using old town plans, photographs, and even 17th-century Canaletto paintings. It has become a symbol of Polish resistance and invincibility. I remember in the 1960s Polish "chronicles", short films screened in cinemas before the main feature, showing smiling, enthusiastic people singing and laying bricks together, one on top of the other. The narrator would announce that yet another Warsaw building had just been resurrected. I thought about these young volunteer builders while sitting in a café in the main square of Warsaw's Old Town (*Stare Miasto*), admiring the town houses around me and finding it difficult to believe that they were built just 50, rather than 200 years ago.

OPPOSITE "The Square by the Royal Castle" (*Krakowskie Przedmieście*) by Bernardo Bellotto (also known as Canaletto II), 1768, Musée du Louvre, Paris. BELOW Tomb of the Unknown Soldier.

Summer in Poland

The royal castle (*Zamek Królewski*) took years to rebuild – the beneficiary of many scout appeals and fundraising campaigns. In primary school, I collected old newspapers (urging my parents and neighbours to read faster) and sold them to raise money for the "Rebuild the Castle Fund". I still remember donating 5 złoty (just a few cents) which I had made from collecting 25 kilos of recycled newspapers (five suitcase-sized bundles carefully bound with string). I got a badge to sew onto my scout uniform in return for my contribution. Looking at the restored castle for the first time today I can now claim a tiny part in its reconstruction. My husband listens sceptically to this story: he never did any reselling of old newspapers at his English school.

We went inside and saw Polish children sigh with amazement at the lavish red, green, and gold royal rooms. Kings and queens from gilded portraits gazed down on them, testing their knowledge of Polish history. "Which King am I?" they seemed to ask.

ABOVE LEFT "The Girl in a Picture Frame" also known as "The Jewish Bride" by Rembrandt, 1641. ABOVE RIGHT "Portrait of Ignacy Jan Paderewski" by Wacław Roman Przybylski.

We sat at the foot of Zygmunt's Column outside the castle, watching the evening crowd gather in the famous square, the *Krakowskie Przedmieście*. I kept thinking about two paintings I had seen inside the castle: Rembrandt's "The Jewish Bride" and the portrait of former Polish Prime Minister, the composer and pianist, Jan Paderewski. Maybe now the castle was empty, Jan Paderewski was sitting at the grand piano in the ballroom playing a Chopin Polonaise for the Jewish bride. I felt sure he was, for soon we could hear piano music coming from across the square.

Summer in Poland

Warsaw by Night

At dusk we took a leisurely walk around the Mermaid Fountain (*Syrenka*) in the *Stare Miasto*. The Old Town was overrun by young people kissing, embracing, holding hands, calling out "I love you", or texting plans to meet later when it was fully dark. Of course they took it for granted that this ancient square, their lovers' playground, was rebuilt just for them by those young, smiling people in the old Polish chronicle films – their grandparents.

We stopped and listened to a live band performing the Eugeniusz Bodo song "I had a date with her at nine" (*Umówiłem się z nią na dziewiątą*). The old but well-known tune made the evening swell with nostalgia and romance as we sat down to dinner on a balmy summer's evening. I kissed my husband when they played Hanka Ordonówna's "Love will forgive you everything" (*Miłość ci wszystko wybaczy*). I knew there was nowhere else in Europe I would rather be on such an enchanted night.

BELOW Eugeniusz Bodo with Helena Grossówna in the 1938 comedy *Paweł i Gaweł*. Bodo was a singer, director, and star of many Polish movies. He opened his own Café Bodo in Warsaw in 1939 where Polish actors and singers continued to perform during the Siege of Warsaw. Bodo was arrested in 1941, deported to Russia, and killed. His cheerful, romantic music can still be heard throughout the capital today, revered by all Poles, whatever their age.

Roast Duck with Apples

 KACZKA PIECZONA Z JABŁKAMI

A popular, traditional Polish dish. It is as simple and easy to roast a duck at home as it is a chicken. Roast duck goes down nicely with a bottle of dry red wine.

SERVES 4

2 kg (4 lb 7 oz) DUCK

2 MEDIUM-SIZED APPLES

2 TABLESPOONS CHOPPED FRESH MARJORAM

3 CLOVES GARLIC, CRUSHED

1 kg (2 lb 3 oz) SMALL POTATOES (ANY TYPE)

1 TABLESPOON CARAWAY SEEDS

Preheat the oven to 240°C (475°F).

Rinse the duck with water and pat dry. Wash, peel, core, and chop the apples into small chunks and stuff the cavity of the duck. Rub the skin well with the marjoram, the garlic, and salt and pepper. Place on a large plate, cover, and leave for 45 minutes to marinate.

Place the duck in a roasting tray. Collect any marinade left in the plate, and add some more water to make up one cup of liquid. Pour this liquid around the duck in the roasting tray – not over it or you will wash off the marinade.

Roast the duck uncovered for 10 minutes, then reduce the heat to 160°C (320°F) and cook for 2 hours. Every half an hour or so use a fine skewer to pierce the duck skin with holes to release its juices and then baste the duck with the liquid that collects in the bottom of the pan.

Clean the potatoes and cut into halves or quarters (there is no need to peel them). When the duck still has about an hour to cook, salt the potatoes, place them in the tray with the duck, and sprinkle with caraway seeds. They should start to fry gently in the duck fat. When you next baste the duck, turn the potatoes, making sure they are well covered with the duck juices. Add another sprinkle of caraway seeds if you like.

The duck should be so well cooked that it can be easily pulled apart and served in chunks. It's no fun trying to carve a duck.

229

Summer in Poland

Ricotta Sultana Crêpes § NALEŚNIKI Z SEREM

The secret to this exquisitely rich dessert is to make a very thin pancake like a French crêpe. You can add more milk or water to the batter if necessary to achieve the right consistency. In Poland sweet pancakes are often served as a main meal.

MAKES 6 PANCAKES

FOR THE FILLING

500 g (1 lb 2 oz) CREAM CHEESE

200 g (7 oz) SULTANAS

110 g (4 oz) CASTER (SUPERFINE) SUGAR

A FEW DROPS VANILLA ESSENCE

ZEST OF 1 LEMON

2 EGG YOLKS

FOR THE PANCAKE MIX

120 ml (4 fl oz) CUP WATER

120 ml (4 fl oz) FULL CREAM MILK

150 g (5 oz) PLAIN (ALL-PURPOSE) FLOUR

4 EGGS

FOR DECORATION

ICING (POWDERED) SUGAR

MANDARIN SEGMENTS, OR OTHER SEASONAL FRUIT

To make the filling, mix the cream cheese with the sultanas, sugar, vanilla essence, lemon zest, and egg yolks until well blended.

To make the pancake mix whisk together the water, milk, flour, and eggs. Melt a little butter in a hot pan and pour in a ladleful of the batter at a time, flipping the pancake over to cook on both sides until golden brown.

Spoon a little filling onto each pancake as it comes out of the pan and fold it into quarters. Decorate with fruit slices and dust with the sugar.

Summer in Poland

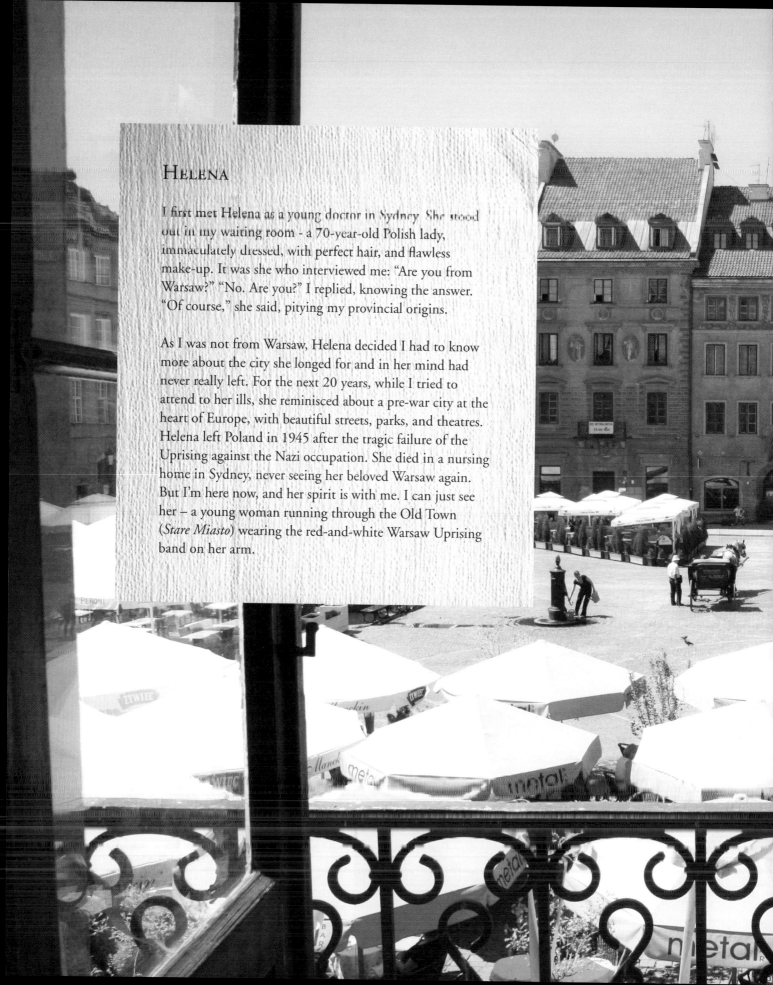

HELENA

I first met Helena as a young doctor in Sydney. She stood out in my waiting room - a 70-year-old Polish lady, immaculately dressed, with perfect hair, and flawless make-up. It was she who interviewed me: "Are you from Warsaw?" "No. Are you?" I replied, knowing the answer. "Of course," she said, pitying my provincial origins.

As I was not from Warsaw, Helena decided I had to know more about the city she longed for and in her mind had never really left. For the next 20 years, while I tried to attend to her ills, she reminisced about a pre-war city at the heart of Europe, with beautiful streets, parks, and theatres. Helena left Poland in 1945 after the tragic failure of the Uprising against the Nazi occupation. She died in a nursing home in Sydney, never seeing her beloved Warsaw again. But I'm here now, and her spirit is with me. I can just see her – a young woman running through the Old Town (*Stare Miasto*) wearing the red-and-white Warsaw Uprising band on her arm.

The Palace of Culture

Built in the 1950s in Stalinist times as a gift from Russia to Poland, Warsaw's Palace of Culture (*Pałac Kultury*) remains the tallest building in the country. All school children had to make the obligatory trip to the terrace on its 30th floor to see the view of our capital. My violin teacher said this monstrous skyscraper was a symbol of Soviet oppression and I ought to despise it, but I found it hard not to get excited as I crammed into the lift with all my classmates for the giddy ride to the top. It was, after all, our Eiffel Tower, and the tallest building any Polish child could conquer.

Every year, the May Day parades that took place in the *Plac Defilad* in front were broadcast round Poland. I had watched a snowy, black-and-white screen showing tired Polish workers marching, waving, and saluting at distant party officials, grateful for a day off from their six-day working week. Yes, I marched too as a ten-year-old scout: red scarf around my neck and giant red crêpe-paper carnation in my hand, I silently prayed that my anti-communist great-grandfather Dimitri would not strike me down from the heavens above.

Now, 35 years later, I looked down at the square below. Today there were no marchers, just giant billboards advertising jeans, stalls selling chocolate waffles, and building cranes splitting the skyline. I gazed down like an omnipotent leader from my tower above and felt great pride for this country, for its true democracy and freedom. No-one is forced into pointless marches any more, no-one compromises their beliefs, fearing for their survival. I waved Warsaw goodbye and saluted its enduring spirit.

Chocolate Waffles § WAFLE CZEKOLADOWE

Many tram stops in Warsaw surprisingly smell of chocolate waffles. We soon found out that the small kiosks that sell tickets, sweets, and magazines also sell chocolate-filled waffles. Stacks of them are displayed behind the kiosks' glass windows and their aroma permeates through morning papers. We just couldn't resist joining other commuters to buy them. It was reassuring to know that wherever the tram took us another kiosk with waffles awaited us.

This is my grandmother Józefa's recipe for chocolate waffles. You can buy sheets of waffle from most delis, so here I have just given the recipe for the filling.

MAKES 1 GIANT WAFFLE THAT CAN BE CUT INTO ABOUT 20 INDIVIDUAL SNACK-SIZED PIECES

2 EGGS

1 EGG YOLK

110 g (4 oz) CASTER (SUPERFINE) SUGAR

1 TEASPOON COCOA POWDER

125 g (5 oz) UNSALTED BUTTER

5 LARGE READY-MADE WAFFLE SHEETS

Mix the eggs and yolk together with the sugar in a *bain marie* over a low heat. Blend in the cocoa powder.

Cut the butter into little pieces and soften, then beat (or use a food processor if you have one) until smooth and creamy. Stir in the egg and sugar mix.

Spread 4 of the 5 waffle sheets with a thin layer of the chocolate filling mix then use these to build up your tower, topping it off with the final waffle sheet. Set aside for a few hours to allow the filling to soak into the waffles, then cut into small strips or squares as you like.

Chopin's House

Fryderyk Chopin's birthplace in the town of Żelazowa Wola is a typical 19th-century, Polish nobleman's homestead or *dworek* (as described in the opening lines of Mickiewicz' epic poem *Pan Tadeusz*). The house is now a museum, set in luscious gardens with a stream full of wavy river weed and blue dragonflies. When we visited a crowd of Polish tourists shuffled respectfully through like pilgrims. The gardens felt contemplative, with music played through loudspeakers hidden in the trees. All the seats and benches were occupied by listeners, mesmerized by mazurkas, polonaises, and études. "Quiet!" I felt like shouting at a noisy magpie.

The live performance that night was sold out. "But we have come all the way from Sydney!" we shamelessly begged, and the attendant kindly let us in. As I listened to the nostalgic music on a dreamy, warm summer's night, I thought Chopin himself would have loved the idea of his nocturnes being performed in the place where he was born. Chopin left Poland in 1830 and never returned. But he created music that could carry any Polish migrant back home, from anywhere in the world, whenever it was played.

238

From "PAN TADEUSZ"

Mid such fields years ago, by the edge of a rill,
In a grove of white birches, upon a slight hill,
Stood a gentleman's manor, of wood, but on stone;
The home's whitewashed walls brightly from faraway shone
Seeming whiter in contrast with dusky green trees,
The poplars, which stood guarding it from autumn's breeze.

Śród takich pól przed laty, nad brzegiem ruczaju,
Na pagórku niewielkim, we brzozowym gaju
Stał dwór szlachecki, z drzewa, lecz podmurowany;
Świeciły się z daleka pobielane ściany,
Tym bielsze, że odbite od ciemnej zieleni
Topoli, co go bronią od wiatrów jesieni.

From *Pan Tadeusz* by Adam Mickiewicz,
Book I: The Estate, Paris, 1834
(trans. Marcel Weyland)

Violin lessons

I was taught violin as a child by a 70-year-old family friend, Zbigniew Górecki. His students called him Uncle Zbyszek (Wujek Zbyszek). My lessons would always start with a cup of tea served in a bone china cup with a golden rim, and sweetened with a spoonful of fruit jam – *konfitury* – from an ornamental silver bowl. Aged ten I thought this was the height of sophistication.

Wujek's family had all perished in Warsaw during the Second World War and in 1945 he had moved west to Jelenia Góra to try to make a living teaching music. But it hadn't been easy. He was jailed for two years in the 1950s for making an anti-Stalin joke while queuing to buy bread. When this stint in jail did not cure his anti-communist views (it only strengthened them) he was barred from teaching in the Music Academy and made to work in the local meat plant instead. Here he soon became very popular among the workers because of his undaunted sense of humour and wit. Soon he was teaching their kids music, Latin, or French. As he had been banned from working as a teacher, he was paid for his lessons in food and knitted jumpers so he could not be accused of running an illegal business. Jars of *konfitury* and *smalec* were piled up on his piano as each student brought a home-cooked gift as admission to his attic studio. Only now I realize he probably could not afford to buy sugar, hence the donated *konfitury* used to sweeten our tea.

As I drank my tea he would report what he had heard on the heavily jammed Radio Free Europe the night before. He would passionately reassure his students about the imminent collapse of communism. We were his young army of Polish dissident violinists ready to attack the regime with our bows.

When frustrated with my playing and lack of practice he would accuse me of "sawing the violin in two". Then he would pick up his own violin to show me how to play properly, and the best part of the lesson would begin. He was no longer in his small attic room but in some pre-war Warsaw concert hall. He played Bach's *Air on a G String* with subtlety and finesse, Paganini's *La Campanella* with Italian fire. But when he played music by the Polish composer Wieniawski with true romantic expression, the music would choke my throat and not let go until he stopped. He would smile and bow at the end, pleased to impress his humble audience. Wujek Zbyszek died in the mid 1980s, shortly before communism came to an end in Poland. I cannot listen to a recording of Wieniawski's *Légende* today with dry eyes, as I think of my legendary violin teacher.

Flavoured Teas

My grandmother used to make me stoppered bottles of black tea to take to school. She would often sweeten them with different jams. It was always a surprise to take a swig and taste peaches, blackberries, or strawberries. Sometimes a whole fruit would sit at the bottom of the bottle or a large sweet strawberry block the neck. I would then have to dig it out with my finger and eat it. My English husband cannot believe that Poles add jam to their tea. I'm not so sure about adding milk, myself.

The following recipes are for hot fruit teas that I still make for my kids at home – they are soothing and, especially the mint tea, good for the digestion.

Apple Tea   HERBATA JABŁKOWA

This is a simple way to use apple peel after you have made apple pancakes (see page 174) or another apple recipe (having scrubbed the apples clean before peeling).

Spread out the peel on baking paper and dry it in an oven on a low heat with the door open.

Once the peelings are brown and brittle crumble them into a clean jar and seal.

Pour boiling water over the crumbled peel and try it sweetened with honey and a dash of cinammon sugar.

Mint Tea   HERBATA MIĘTOWA

You will need to infuse about 2 tablespoons of chopped fresh mint leaves for 2 cups of tea.

Pour boiling water onto the mint, cover, and allow to steep for 5–10 minutes. Pour into cups, straining as you go.

The Heart of Poland

We headed south east of Warsaw through Mazovia, Podlasie, and Lubelskie. Driving through a labyrinth of country roads we collected blessings for a safe journey from roadside saints, whose solemn statues guarded crossings, junctions, and bridges. We followed only one rule: if we got stuck behind a giant truck on its way to the border we would take the first exit, whether right or left, and find our way along the tiny back roads on our Tesco map.

Our rule paid off, as within minutes of leaving the highway we were invariably greeted by fields of wildflowers, and music performed by a regional assembly of frogs and birds. We gave way to all sorts of creatures: birds, cows, and goats. On one occasion we stopped to let a flock of local ducks cross the road. They glanced sideways at our headlights with the same superior expression you see on the faces of sailors in Sydney Harbour, when motor is forced to give way to sail.

Sometimes the route became a dirt track ending somewhere, nowhere. One afternoon we arrived unexpectedly in the middle of a blossoming potato field. The dark asphalt road that on our map showed every promise of continuing stopped abruptly, giving in to an ocean of white flowers that

swayed gently in a hay-scented wind. We decided to picnic here before asking a local saint where we were. St Kazimierz, who watched over the crops from his plaster shrine, urged us to stop rushing, lie down on the ground, and watch the passing clouds for further directions.

For the next days and weeks we were drawn into dark green forests and secret leafy passages, emerging every now and then to visit yet another historic city in the heart of Poland... the craft centre Łowicz, riverside Kazimierz Dolny, or Renaissance Zamość... only to disappear again, among dark summer trees in search of a greener than green universe.

From "SONG OF THE
INEXHAUSTIBLE SUN"

Supposing this cosmos is a branch
bent by its leafy weight,
and sunshine washes over it.
Supposing each gaze is a quiet deep
held in the palm of the hand –

Though leaves tremble, though they fall,
their reflection somewhere near,
the quiet deep will always keep
its gaze on You. The Hidden.

Jeśli ten kosmos jest gałęzią ciężką liści,
którą opływa światło słońca,
jeśli spojrzenie jest tonią spokojną,
zaczerpniętą na otwartą dłoń –

Więc chociaż liście drżą i opadają,
w niedalekiej głębi odbite,
toń spokojna się ciągle wpatruje
w Ciebie – Ukryty.

Karol Wojtyła (Pope John Paul II), 1979

Łowicz

We knew we were in Łowicz as soon as we saw the striped fabric in bright green, pink, black, and red – *pasiaki* – typical of this region. Made for traditional costumes and decoration it was on display in shops and churches everywhere. Łowicz is not only the geographical heart of Poland, but also the epicentre of Poland's folkloric arts and crafts, and in particular paper cutting.

A craft shop owner assured us it was easy to make your own intricate paper designs. She folded a round piece of paper into four and rapidly made a series of small cuts and holes. When she unfolded it the result was miraculous: two mirror-imaged roosters, facing each other. We soon realized we might need more than one lesson to learn how to do this, and decided to buy some ready-made cuttings. We could always claim them as our own work when we got home.

249

Summer Gardens

In much of Poland, only the rich or lazy buy vegetables at the supermarket. As soon as the snow melts in spring, those who live in tiny, communist-built apartments spill out into their own summer gardens, special "grow-your-own" allotments known as *działki* (roughly pronounced *jow-kee*). Here every centimetre of soil is cultivated with gooseberries, potatoes, chives, cabbages, and a thousand flowers. *Działki* are maintained with fierce pride and the same ingenious use of space you find in the small apartments. Old garden sheds become romantic gazebos, a patch of grass under an apple tree the perfect place for a Sunday family lunch. Weeds are picked by hand, and only "occasionally" thrown onto the neighbours allotment when no-one is looking. Always an important source of fresh parsley, dill, and cucumbers, *działki* offer a quiet place for adults to contemplate the passing seasons and for kids to grow like unruly beansprouts.

250

BESIDE THE FENCE...

Near the fence long mounds, convex, with greenery filled,
Without tree, bush or flower the cucumber hill
Growing gloriously, large-leafed and broadly outspread,
Like a rich verdant carpet they covered the bed.

POD PŁOTEM WĄSKIE...

Pod płotem wąskie, długie, wypukłe pagórki
Bez drzew, krzewów i kwiatów: ogród na ogórki.
Pięknie wyrosły; liściem wielkim, rozłożystym,
Okryły grzędy jakby kobiercem fałdzistym.

From *Pan Tadeusz* by Adam Mickiewicz,
Book II: The Castle, Paris, 1834
(trans. Marcel Weyland)

White Cabbage and Carrot Salad

§ SURÓWKA Z BIAŁEJ KAPUSTY Z MARCHEWKĄ

This crisp salad is the true taste of summer – if you can find the freshest of ingredients to make it.

MAKES A SIDE SALAD FOR 4 OR A MAIN DISH FOR 2

½ SAVOY CABBAGE

1 APPLE

1 CARROT

½ ONION

1 TEASPOON LEMON JUICE

1 TEASPOON OLIVE OIL

1 TEASPOON CASTER (SUPERFINE) SUGAR

1 TABLESPOON CARAWAY SEEDS (OPTIONAL)

Slice and chop the cabbage and onion very finely, almost as if it has been grated.

Peel the apple and carrot, then grate both. Mix all the ingredients lightly together.

Make a dressing by whisking or shaking together in a bottle the lemon juice, olive oil, and sugar. Season with salt and pepper, then add to the salad and dress by tossing.

My mother Lidia sometimes stirs in a tablespoon of caraway seeds, for added flavour.

Red Cabbage Salad

§ SURÓWKA Z CZERWONEJ KAPUSTY

This is similar to the white cabbage salad above, but uses red cabbage, softened with salt.

MAKES ENOUGH FOR 4 AS A SIDE SALAD

1 SMALL RED CABBAGE

1 SMALL RED ONION

1 APPLE, PEELED

1 TEASPOON CASTER (SUPERFINE) SUGAR

1 TABLESPOON OLIVE OIL

JUICE OF ½ LEMON

GOOD PINCH OF SALT

Shred the cabbage then sprinkle with the salt and mix well. Let it stand for half an hour for the red cabbage to soften.

Chop the onion finely and grate the apple. Add both to the cabbage.

Stir together well with the oil, sugar, and lemon juice and season with pepper.

Carrot and Sultana Salad

§ SURÓWKA Z MARCHEWKI Z RODZYNKAMI

This recipe is always popular with children, because of its bright colour, sweetness – and added sultanas.

MAKES ENOUGH FOR 4 AS A SIDE SALAD

2 LARGE CARROTS

1 LARGE APPLE

2 TABLESPOONS SULTANAS (OR GOLDEN RAISINS)

1 TEASPOON LEMON JUICE

½ TEASPOON CASTER (SUPERFINE) SUGAR (OPTIONAL, IF CARROTS AND APPLES NEED SWEETENING)

1 TABLESPOON LIGHT OR SINGLE CREAM (OPTIONAL)

Peel then grate the apples and carrots. Mix them together well with a teaspoon of lemon juice and the sultanas.

For a more indulgent version, stir in one tablespoon of fresh cream and half a teaspoon of caster (superfine) sugar.

Zamość

ZAMOŚĆ

Summer in Poland

Jan Zamoyski was a man with a dream: to build a perfect, Renaissance city at the crossroads linking north-west Europe with the Black Sea. Zamoyski was Chancellor of Poland during King Stefan Batory's reign. A patron of the arts and sciences, by 1600 he and his Italian architect Bernardo Morando had completed their ideal city: Zamość.

Some 400 years later we drove into this Italianate town on the far eastern border of Poland. We ambled through the shady arcades that make up Zamość's centre, enjoying a lesson in Renaissance town design. Some of the merchant houses above us had been built by Armenians, one of the many ethnic groups – including Greeks, Jews, Germans, Italians, English, and Dutch – drawn to this cosmopolitan city over the centuries.

Though it was midsummer, few tourists walked with us that Saturday afternoon and there was no pressure to hurry round the many sights. We booked a room overlooking the main town square and watched the half dozen weddings that took place on the steps of the distinguished town hall

(*ratusz*). We sipped champagne while sitting in our window, feeling a little like gatecrashers, toasting grooms and brides we had never met.

We walked to Zamenhofa Street to see the old Renaissance synagogue built by Sephardic Jews from Venice. As we went in we stepped down – the floor had been cleverly lowered to increase the height of the interior room. Sunshine poured through the high windows, casting a long shadow of the Star of David across the old, stone floor.

The same sun poured into the town's catholic cathedral, where we found Zamoyski's tomb in a side chapel. The Renaissance statue of this generous, Polish patriot, lying down for his eternal sleep, was touching. We climbed the tower to appreciate Morando's geometrical city design with a bird's eye view.

Summer in Poland

Infamous tongue twister

In Zamość we passed a sign for Szczebrzeska Street (pronounced "Sh-cheb-zhesca Street"). It reminded me of Jan Brzechwa's famous tongue twister, and provided a wonderful opportunity to torture Simon as we drove.

"You try and say it", I said gently to Mr "I went to Cambridge and Know Absolutely Everything". "It's easy really, Szczebrzeszyn. Sh for Shakespeare, Ch for Chekhov…"

Simon hissed and whistled and screwed up his face but couldn't do it. In the end he sulked and made me drive.

This is the infamous tongue twister about a beetle in the reeds (which manages to stick together all the difficult Polish consonants, creating the sound of a buzzing insect).

In Szczebrzeszyn a cricket buzzes in the reeds	*W Szczebrzeszynie chrząszcz brzmi w trzcinie*
Szczebrzeszyn is famous for it	*i Szczebrzeszyn z tego słynie*
An ox asks him: "Mister cricket,	*Wół go pyta: "Panie chrząszczu,*
Why are you buzzing in the thicket?"	*Po cóż pan tak brzęczy w gąszczu?"*

Jan Brzechwa was one of my favourite childhood authors and I spent long hours in the summer reading his *Pan Kleks* stories. Pan Kleks (Mr Inkblot) was headmaster of a magical academy, long before Harry Potter was born. Like other characters from childrens' stories, his picture appeared in the 1960s on chocolate bar wrappers, the chocolates piled up in perfect helices in the glass windows of sweet shops. When I had finally saved up enough pocket money and ran enthusiastically to buy some the shop assistant would remove the top bar of chocolate with perfect precision, without disturbing the helix. I harboured a secret wish that the stack would collapse, and all the chocolate bars break inside their wrappers. Then the damaged goods would have to be given away free – to me – the only child in Poland happy to eat broken chocolate.

JAN BRZECHWA

Pan
KLEKS

ilustrował
J. M. SZANCER

Our favourite summer aperitif on tour was apple juice and *Żubrówka* ("bison vodka"). The vodka is so-called as it contains a blade of grass from the Białowieża Forest, where wild bison love to eat the grass. The aperitif tastes like apple pie, hence its nickname – *szarlotka* ("Charlotte-kah"). Half and half on ice is all you need to make *szarlotka*. The size of the glass is up to you.

264

ABOVE Niedzica Castle. OPPOSITE
Czorsztyn Castle.

Castles on the Border

The castles of Czorsztyn and Niedzica face each other across Czorsztyn
Lake: two ancient fortresses, guarding their steep shores. Pedalos and
yachts now skated across the mirrored surface of the lake without a wave
or sound. The evening sun meddled with the green and blues of the water
turning it bright orange, against all the rules of colour mixing. The ripples
from my plunging pebble spread like radio waves with the news that some
sentimental woman, too old to be playing skipping stones, was scaring the
dragonflies on Czorsztyn Lake.

Tatra Mountains

Summer in Poland

The peaks of Tatra, the highest range of the Carpathian mountains, are often hidden in cloud. The steep slopes are challenging to climb – but seem no obstacle to mountain goats or Polish children. Groups of kids kept overtaking us as we tried to reach the closest summit, *Kasprowy Wierch*. Each time these show-offs ran past us they called out "Hello!" before disappearing into the dark, ancient forest ahead. We stopped smiling when they had passed, and collapsed exhausted to the ground, ignoring the daisies and forget-me-nots sticking into our nostrils. There's been a cable car to the top since 1935, one of the oldest in Europe. We wished we had taken it, and forgone the authentic mountaineering experience.

Halfway up the mountain we followed a narrow track, winding among moss-covered pines and oaks, and came upon a small wooden monastery. The outside chapel was left open for any visitors but the monastery doors were firmly shut. We read the information posted on the door about the order of monks who reside here, isolated from the world, requesting all

outsiders to respect it. We sat in front of the chapel enjoying the serene atmosphere and the chance to stop walking but our bliss was soon interrupted by a loud banging noise. An old woman who had just arrived on the scene was rapping her walking stick on the massive monastery door. This was going to be interesting. After a while the door slowly opened and a young, pale, ascetic-looking man appeared, his ivory hands clutching the ebony door handles. We couldn't hear what the woman wanted but the monk seemed unperturbed. He withdrew into the darkness then returned with a glass of water. No escape from the outside world in the 21st century we concluded, with quiet satisfaction.

Carpathian Vanilla Torte § KARPATKA

Karpatku is made from sheets of puff pastry filled with vanilla cream. When cooked the pastry bubbles up with a wavy contour like the Carpathian mountains, hence its name. This is only for those who are prepared to burn off the extra calories climbing mountains.

The pastry should be especially light and fluffy…

MAKES ENOUGH FOR 10

1 CUP WATER

110 g (4 oz) UNSALTED BUTTER

PINCH OF SALT

150 g (5 oz) PLAIN (ALL-PURPOSE) FLOUR

5 EGGS

1 TEASPOON BAKING POWDER

FOR THE VANILLA-CREAM FILLING

350 ml (12 fl oz) MILK

170 g (6 oz) CASTER (SUPERFINE) SUGAR

50 g (2 oz) VANILLA SUGAR

50 g (2 oz) PLAIN FLOUR (ALL-PURPOSE) FLOUR (WHEAT NOT RYE)

50 g (2 oz) POTATO FLOUR

375 g (13 oz) UNSALTED BUTTER

ICING (POWDERED) SUGAR, FOR DUSTING

Preheat the oven to 240°C (475°F).

Mix the water, butter, and salt together and heat gently in a saucepan.

Mix in the flour. Keep stirring the dough gently – the pastry will lift off the bottom of the saucepan when it is ready.

Set aside to cool a little, then add the eggs one by one and keep stirring. Once the eggs are blended in, fold in the baking powder.

Line 2 square tins 25 x 25 x 5 cm (10 x 10 x 2 in) with ungreased baking paper.

Divide the pastry into 2 equal parts, rolling out each part on a floured board until it is very just a few mm thick – ¼ in – to fit each prepared tin.

Bake for 20 minutes or until golden brown. It will bubble up like the wavy horizon of the Carpathian Mountains.

TO MAKE THE VANILLA-CREAM FILLING

Heat two-thirds of the milk with all the sugar in a saucepan until bubbling.

Sift together both the flours and slowly add the remaining milk, mixing to a smooth paste. Then add it to the saucepan, stirring vigorously to ensure there are no lumps. Leave to cool.

Cream the butter in a food processor until smooth, adding the milk and flour mix as you go.

Cover one pastry square with all the cream filling, then remove the other square of pastry from its tin, take off the baking paper, and place it on top.

Dust with the icing sugar and serve.

Zakopane

Zakopane, a small town in the Tatra mountains, has been a destination for poets, painters, and composers for centuries. It is a Polish Mount Parnassus where divine inspiration descends from cloudy mountain peaks, down steep chalet roofs to flowery meadows, straight into the fertile minds of artists. This, for example, was how the *Stabat Mater,* composed in heaven and full of mountain folk tunes, came to be written down by Karol Szymanowski, a resident composer of Zakopane at the beginning of the 20th century.

Like Venetian gondoliers, mountain men (*Górale*) in traditional costumes wait to ferry tourists in horse-drawn carts from the bottom of the cable car back to their chalets. Poles love the *Górale,* an ethnic group unique to

OPPOSITE Mountain cheeses: *Bryndza* cheese is made from local sheep's milk, dried in the sun. It is soft and crumbly, with a slightly grainy texture and a strong flavour. *Oscypek* is the smoked version. Smooth and mild, and also made from sheep's milk, it is moulded into different shapes from barrels to spaghetti-like strands.

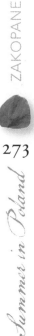

this mountainous region. Their language and culture are a bottomless well for Polish humour and aphorisms. Whenever I saw a *Góral* I couldn't help thinking of Janosik, my favourite TV character from the 1970s – a Polish Robin Hood – from Tatra, rather than Sherwood Forest.

We strolled through the town markets past mountains of *bryndza* (cheese made out of sheeps' milk) and *oscypek* (smoked cheese shaped into little barrel shapes). Traditional walking sticks – *ciupagi* – were on sale, as well as metal badges with etchings of each mountain peak waiting to be climbed.

It may have been summer but unpredictable temperatures and strong winds made restaurants and taverns a cosy port of call, and hot wine an essential refreshment. The café under the cable car station had a special "meal deal" on offer. Large illuminated displays advertised a Polish "Happy Meal": eight *pierogi* and a carton of orange juice for 8 złoty (a couple of dollars). There was a long queue despite no free toy, fries, or upsizing on offer. Homemade and freshly cooked, this was fast food worth a long wait.

273

Pork with Caraway and Onion

 PIECZEŃ WIEPRZOWA Z KMINKIEM I CEBULĄ

Another traditional Polish standard… and a very simple recipe to make. If you have a camp oven or heavy lidded pot, you can cook this out of doors on an open fire, having first marinated the meat in your kitchen at home. It would be a hearty meal after a day in the mountains.

SERVES 6

1 kg (2 lb 3 oz) PORK NECK FILLET

SALT AND PEPPER

2 TABLESPOONS CARAWAY SEEDS

2 ONIONS

Preheat the oven to 180°C (350°F).

Score the meat (to help it absorb the condiments) then rub salt, pepper, and caraway seeds into the pork. Leave for half an hour to marinate.

Pour a little olive oil into a heavy-based pan or Dutch oven and seal the meat on all sides on a high heat. Remove the pan from the heat.

Peel the onions, cut into rough chunks, and sprinkle over the meat. Add half a cup of water, cover, and cook in the oven for 40 minutes.

Once cooked, take the pork out and let it stand for 5 minutes before slicing and serving with mashed potato and/or red cabbage *surówka* (see page 254).

Potato Pancakes with Sour Cream

§ PLACKI ZIEMNIACZANE

Potato pancakes, or *placki*, are a perfect snack for hungry hikers. In fact the higher your altitude, the better they taste. Potato pancakes can be enjoyed on their own, served with a little sour cream, or you can make a more substantial dish by adding some meat sauce.

MAKES ENOUGH FOR 4

1 kg (2 lb 3 oz) POTATOES

1 LARGE ONION

2 EGGS

180 ml (6 fl oz) SOUR CREAM, TO SERVE

Wash and peel the uncooked potatoes. Chop the onion roughly then put everything in a food processor with the eggs and season with pepper and salt. Blend until creamy, like a pancake batter.

Fry dollops of the potato mix in a little olive oil in a frying pan or skillet for a couple of minutes on each side.

Serve with sour cream or, for a really filling meal, a meat sauce (see Polish Beef Goulash, page 104).

Summer in Poland

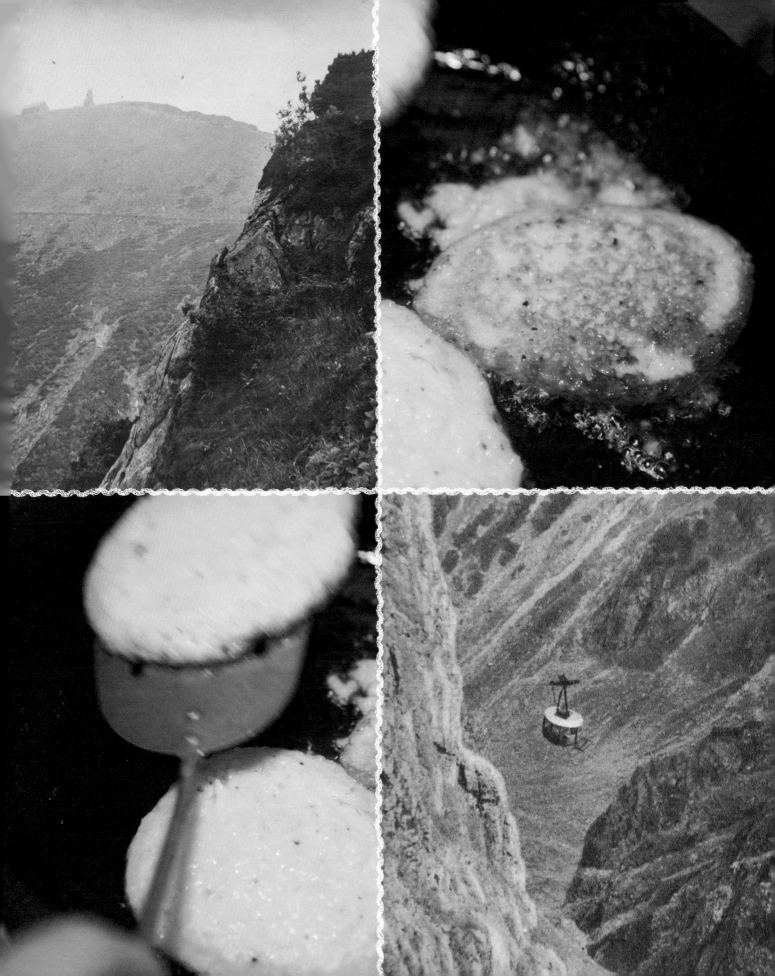

Pork and Cabbage "Hunter's Stew" § BIGOS

This is a Polish staple dish eaten in every region of the country and is made with pork, prunes, cabbage, and sausage. It is often enjoyed out of doors when camping or on hikes in summer. It can be frozen and warmed up in batches as you need it. We made *bigos* using jars of ready-made sauerkraut, dried porcini mushrooms, and smoked garlic sausages.

MAKES ENOUGH FOR 4–6

2 kg (4 lb 7 oz) PICKLED CABBAGE (SAUERKRAUT)

6 DRIED PORCINI MUSHROOMS

500 g (1 lb 2 oz) PORK NECK FILLET

1 SMALL ONION

2 SMOKED SAUSAGES (c500 g (c1 lb))

6 PORK SPARE RIBS (SMOKED)

400 g (14 oz) SOFT, PITTED PRUNES

Empty the sauerkraut into a saucepan and blanch with boiling water. Drain, then rinse the sauerkraut in a colander under the cold tap.

Put the dried mushrooms in a saucepan and cover with cold water. Leave to soak for an hour, then bring to the boil and simmer with a pinch of salt for 15 minutes.

Chop the pork into 3 cm (1 in) cubes and fry in a little olive oil until golden brown.

Chop the onion and fry with the pork for a few minutes until soft. Cut the sausages into 1 cm (½ in) thick slices and fry for a minute or 2 each side.

Combine the sausage, pork, and onion with the cabbage, add salt and pepper to season, and also add the spare ribs and prunes.

Drain the mushrooms, slice finely, and add to the pot. Stir it all together, cover, and cook on a low heat for at least an hour until the cabbage is quite soft.

Serve outside in summer with a hunk of fresh bread and a glass of beer.

Kraków

In Kraków the cucumber season – the sleepy part of summer when there is nothing to do but "watch cucumbers grow" – had been officially cancelled. Nowadays the theatres remain open all July and August, offering different performances every day. Giant round poster columns directed us like road-signs in the wilderness: north for Ibsen at 5.30pm, East for Chekhov at 6pm, West for Brecht, and South for Ionesco. No time to get bored here, Kraków is Poland's mecca for thespians. The summer must be spent in the theatre, rather than frivolously splashing around in the Baltic Sea.

The huge Market Square (*Rynek Główny*), the largest medieval town square in Europe, is definitely the main stage for impromptu performance. There are magicians and fortune tellers, knights in armour, and fire eaters that light up the square. If you are not satisfied with all the theatre (straight or street) there are concerts, opera, underground jazz clubs, cabaret, poetry readings, and more.

Kraków, once the home of Polish Pope John Paul II, is also crowded with churches and convents and there are many young nuns and priests walking briskly about. Not used to seeing clergy on the street, Simon thought they were extras in costume for some movie being made, and he kept looking for the camera crew.

Kraków is an old university town: the Jagiellonian University opened its doors back in the 14th century. Its most famous student was the young Nicolaus Copernicus. The city still belongs to students: in cosy city cafés everywhere they chat, study, and eat sausages and bagels. Their exam results are unforgivingly posted along the university walls for all to see.

And there is music everywhere, from the high voices of ascetic Christian choirs to European punk performers with electric keyboards. Listening to one pair of virtuoso Ukrainian accordionists you could be forgiven for believing that all music was first written for the accordion. Precocious children stunned the crowds with their talent: one dark-haired virtuoso was so young and tiny she could have fitted in her own violin case. All this music kept time to the constant beat of horses' hooves, as they trotted across medieval paving, with tourists bouncing behind in open carriages.

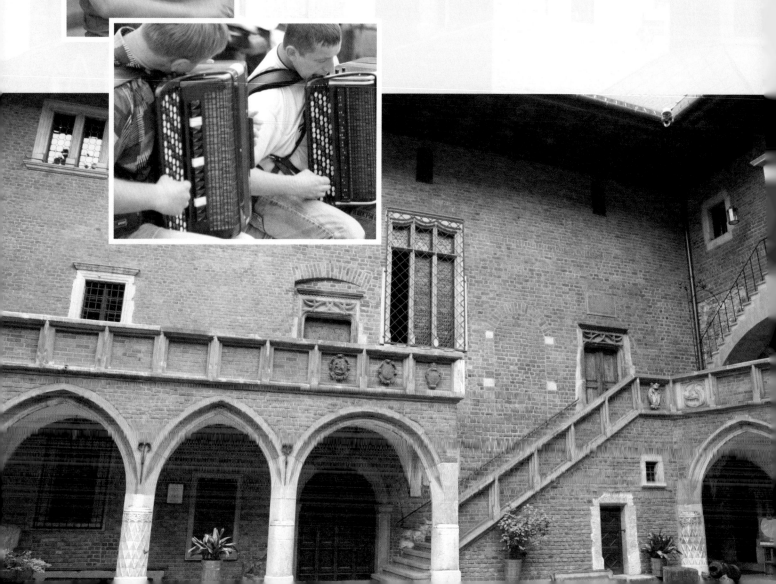

NOWA PROWI

Cabbage Rolls § GOŁĄBKI

We ate *gołąbki* at one of the many outdoor restaurants that spread out into Kraków's main square. These tasty cabbage rolls of rice and meat, served with a tangy tomato sauce and mashed potato, were always popular at my grandmother's home. Making *gołąbki* was a family affair with everyone helping to fold the cabbage leaves. Mountains of cabbage parcels would happily steam away on the stove, making me hungry and impatient to try one.

MAKES 18 ROLLS, ENOUGH FOR 6

200 g (7 oz) LONG GRAIN RICE

2 LARGE ONIONS

1.2 kg (2 lb 12 oz) MINCED BEEF, VEAL, OR PORK (PORK NECK OR RUMP)

1 WHOLE WHITE CABBAGE

1 TABLESPOON BUTTER

FOR THE TOMATO SAUCE

4 TOMATOES

2 TABLESPOONS CONCENTRATED TOMATO PASTE

200 ml (7 fl oz) SINGLE OR PURE CREAM

1 VEGETABLE STOCK (BOUILLON) CUBE

2 TABLESPOONS PLAIN (ALL-PURPOSE) FLOUR

Cook the rice according to the instructions on the packet and drain.

Chop the onions finely and fry them in a little butter until transparent. Mix the mince, onions, and rice together and season with salt and pepper.

Soften the cabbage leaves by boiling the whole cabbage in a large saucepan of water for 5–10 minutes, turning occasionally. Drain and carefully peel off the leaves, keeping them whole. Use a sharp knife to cut out any thick white veins.

Place about a tablespoon of the mince and rice mixture on each cabbage leaf, then wrap the leaf around a couple of times to make a little parcel. Keep a few cabbage leaves back to line the saucepan.

Put a tablespoon of olive oil and about 1 cm (½ in) of water in a large saucepan. Line the pan with 2 or 3 cabbage leaves, then add the wrapped parcels. Add the butter and cover with another layer of cabbage leaves.

Pour in 200 ml (7 fl oz) of cold water then cover and bring to the boil, then lower the heat so it gently simmers for 1 ½ hours (you are steaming the cabbage rolls).

Remove the cooked rolls and pour off 500 ml (17 fl oz) of the liquid into a small saucepan to make the sauce. Add the tomatoes, tomato paste, and cream and heat together gently, mashing the tomatoes with a fork so they break down.

Mix the flour with a little water into a paste and add to the sauce to thicken it, stirring to keep it smooth. Season with a pinch of salt and pepper or sprinkle in a stock cube to taste.

To serve place 2 or 3 *gołąbki* on each plate, then pour over the tomato sauce at the table.

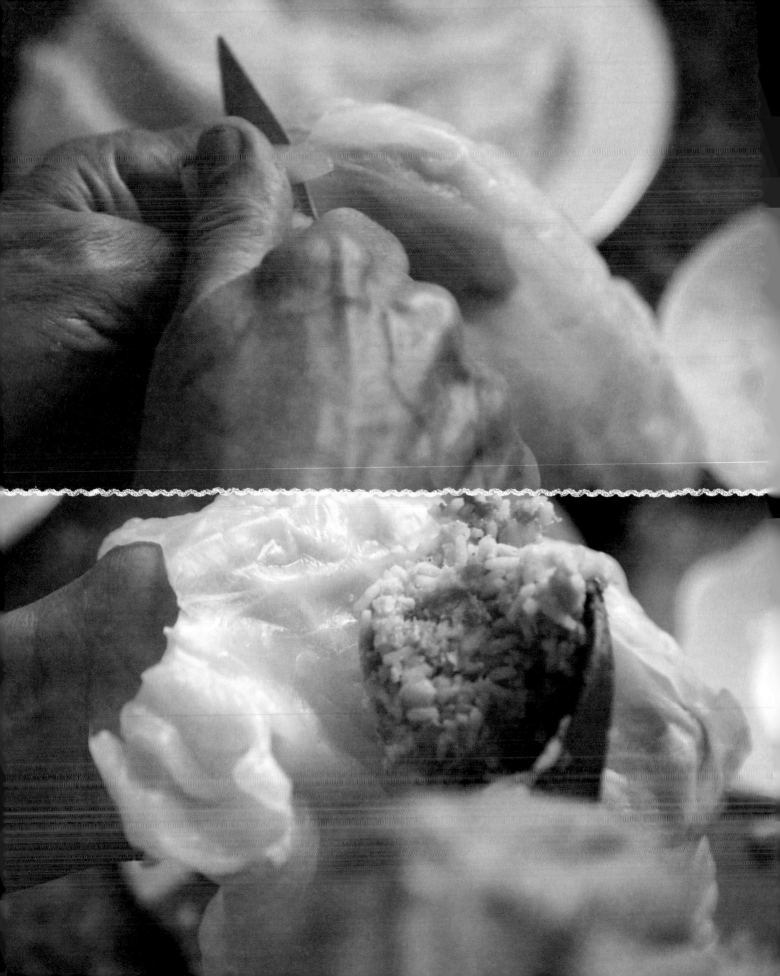

Keeping time

Every hour of every day the cacophony in Kraków's main square stops when a trumpeter standing atop one of the twin towers of the Mariacki Church plays a brief tune – the famous *Hejnał* (pronounced "hey now"). Like a referee in a football match he calls Kraków to order. Tourists gaze, amazed at the gold instrument held against a perfect blue sky, and even locals stare as if looking at this magic vision for the very first time. Legend says that many centuries ago a young trumpeter spotted barbarian invaders heading to attack Kraków. He climbed to the top of one of the towers to trumpet a warning. He was only halfway through when a barbarian arrow pierced his throat, since which time the *Hejnał* stops abruptly before the final note.

You did not have to live in Kraków to hear the *Hejnał*. It was broadcast on the radio each day at noon. Its cheery sound mixed with cosmic radio hiss drifted across our village, through open doors and windows, signalling a three-course lunch with an afternoon rest to follow. The *Hejnał* marked the middle of my impossibly long childhood days, when time dragged, refusing to carry me into adolescence. Oh paradise lost!

OPPOSITE Photograph taken by Beata's father Grzegorz in 1949 of St Mary's Church (*Kościół Mariacki*). The altarpiece inside is by Wit Stwosz.

Kazimierz

We walked through Kazimierz, Kraków's traditional Jewish quarter, with its tiny restaurants and galleries, and street markets selling summer fruit. We sat quietly during a ceremony in the Remuh prayer house, then placed rocks on tombstones in the cemetery behind.

After spending a sunny August afternoon exploring Kazimierz, gazing at the new shops, testing food in cafés, passing men in yarmulkas, I was thrilled to see that Jews and their culture are at last returning where they always belonged, to the medieval streets of Kraków, and hopefully to the rest of Poland as well. *Matzo* soup and *pierogi* on the same menu again.

CHAJIM KOHAN

SKŁAD TOWARÓW RÓŻNYCH

JACEK
DYBEK
Swing

Jacek Dybek ts-cl Audrey Nowak (key)
CZWARTEK (THURSDAY) godz. 40⁰⁰
Dawno temu na Kazimierzu ul. Szeroka 1

Matzo Soup § ZUPA MATZO

Matzo soup consists of a clear chicken broth served with dumplings. The dumplings are made of matzo meal, or ground up matzo bread. Traditionally, matzo balls are bound together with chicken fat skimmed off the top of chicken soup (*schmaltz*) but I prefer the lighter taste of olive oil.

SERVES 4–6

2 l (4 pints) GOOD CHICKEN STOCK

300 g (11 oz) COARSE MATZO MEAL

1–2 TEASPOONS SALT

½ TEASPOON BLACK PEPPER

500 ml (17 fl oz) BOILING WATER

2 LARGE EGGS

1 LARGE ONION, CHOPPED AND FRIED IN A TABLESPOON OF OLIVE OIL

2 TABLESPOONS OLIVE OIL

½ SMALL BUNCH CURLY OR ENGLISH PARSLEY, FINELY CHOPPED

First prepare a batch of chicken stock (see page 154).

Place the matzo meal in a bowl with salt and pepper, pour over the boiling water, and stir it together.

Whisk the eggs, olive oil, and parsley and add to the matzo mix when it has cooled a little. Mix in the chopped fried onion, then refrigerate for at least an hour.

Wet your hands and form the mix into balls; their size is up to you.

Bring the chicken stock to the boil, then reduce to a simmer. Drop the balls into the simmering stock and simmer for at least 20 minutes. Gently turn them while cooking.

Serve with 1 dumpling in each bowl of soup, or 2 if you want to spoil someone.

293

Summer in Poland

Pierogi with Sour Cherries

§ PIEROGI Z WIŚNIAMI

Every restaurant in Kazimierz was competing to serve the best *pierogi* in town – heaven for a *pierogi*-lover like me. I was happy to test all these competing claims. After savoury *pierogi* for lunch, I had *pierogi* with sour cherries for tea. I chose to forget how many I ate and where, but it was an unforgettable afternoon.

Pierogi can be made as a dessert dish, with fresh summer fruits as the filling: strawberries, raspberries, cherries, and blueberries are all good. This recipe uses sour cherries, but you can use sweet cherries (and less sugar) if you prefer.

ENOUGH FOR 60 PIEROGI

TO MAKE THE PASTRY

500 g (1 lb 2 oz) PLAIN (ALL-PURPOSE) FLOUR

50 g (2 oz) UNSALTED BUTTER

250 ml (8 fl oz) WARM WATER

TO MAKE THE CHERRY FILLING

500 g (1 lb 2 oz) RIPE SOUR CHERRIES

110 g (4 oz) CASTER (SUPERFINE) SUGAR (50 g IF USING SWEET CHERRIES)

WHIPPED CREAM, TO SERVE

To make the pastry, first soften the butter in the microwave or leave it out of the fridge for a while. Pile the flour onto a large wooden board, then slowly work in the butter with your fingers. Add the warm water, little by little, to make a soft, elastic dough. Place it in a bowl and cover with a clean tea or dish towel so it doesn't dry out while you are preparing the filling.

To make the cherry filling, wash and stone the cherries before chopping them and mashing them together with a little sugar. Depending on how ripe your cherries are, you will probably need all 100 g (4 oz) of sugar, but if they are well-ripened and quite sweet less will suffice.

Roll out the pastry on the wooden board to about 3 mm (⅛ in) thick. Cut out circles roughly 8 cm (3 in) in diameter using an inverted tumbler and lay them on a floured wooden board, again covered with a cloth until you are ready to fill them.

Place a teaspoon of the sour-cherry filling on each circle of pastry, fold it in half, and carefully close it, crimping the pastry together at the edges with your fingers.

Throw the *pierogi* into a big pot of boiling water. Let them boil for a couple of minutes then take them out and allow to drain.

Serve with whipped cream and caster (superfine) sugar.

Wawel Castle

When Poland regained independence in 1918, Poles all around the world contributed generously to the restoration of Wawel Castle, and their names are immortalized on the wall outside. Kraków was Poland's capital until the end of the 16th century and the castle has always been a symbol of an independent and powerful Polish monarchy in Europe.

A statue of Kościuszko greets visitors to the castle. Tadeusz Kościuszko was the great Polish general who fought in the American War of Independence and led an uprising in Poland in 1794 against Tsarist Russia, with a legendary victory at Racławice. A celebrated hero in Poland and the USA there are statues of him in both countries.

Kościuszko (*Cosh-chuss-co*) is a hard name for non-Poles to pronounce. Polish explorer Strzelecki (another tricky one: *st-she-lets-kee*) named Australia's highest mountain after his hero Kościuszko – condemning generations of Australians to mispronounce one of their country's most famous landmarks (*cossie-osko* and *strez-leckee*). For someone who still struggles to sound "Aussie" it's a great pleasure to correct my fellow Australians.

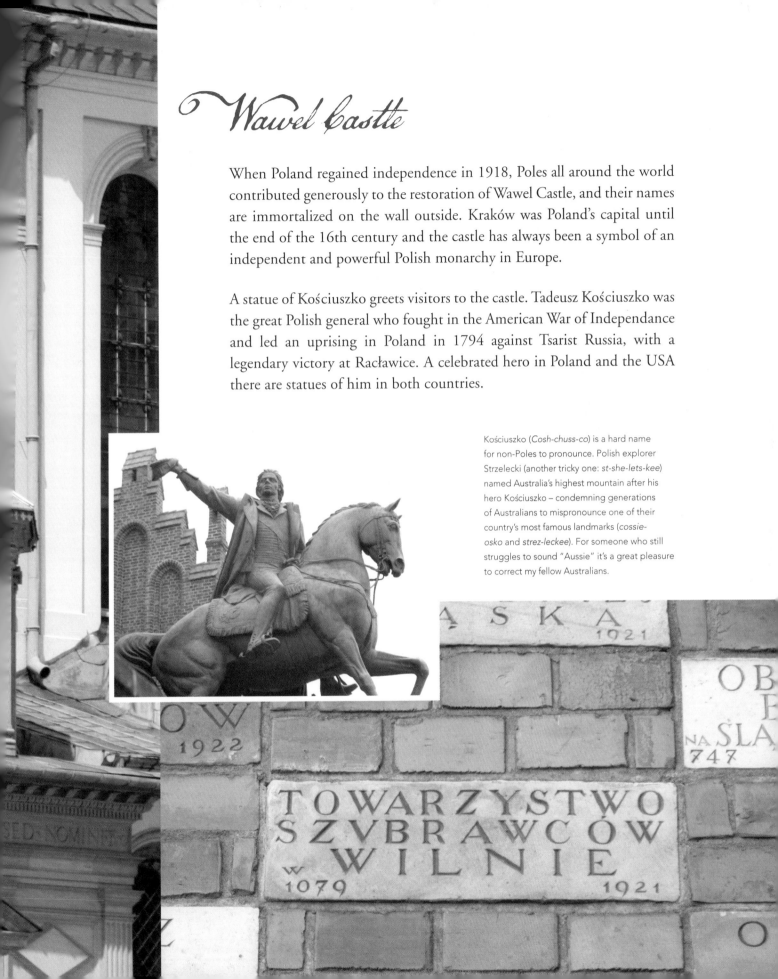

Memories for Sale

I looked wistfully at the arcade of shops in the old Draper's Hall (*Sukiennice*). The traditional folk costume for Cracovian girls, the *strój krakowski*, was for sale. When I was five I longed for a folk outfit like this: full skirt, embroidered bodice with bright ribbons, dazzling sequins sewn into thick velvet, I could not imagine anything more beautiful. I spun round in that skirt many times in my dreams. But it was always too expensive, not suitable, a waste of money, and so on. Like many childhood desires it remained an unfulfilled dream.

I walked into a music shop in the city centre: dark and quiet, an old store, old recordings, old shop assistants. I found many treasures: Polish jazz CDs, Simon Rattle conducting Szymanowski, 1960s and 1970s music, and TV cabaret shows. The 80-year-old shop assistant patiently added up the mounting total on gridlined paper with a sharp pencil, as I used to do in primary school, in pre-calculator days. Finally, when I had bought my luggage limit in CDs, he tore off the bottom corner of the paper where he'd written the total. He then passed it to an even older man sitting in a booth, who looked like Beethoven. I leaned towards a circle cut into the thick glass window. Beethoven looked at me sharply and yelled out the sum I owed. Cash only, no plastic-money nonsense here.

I was charmed, but not wanting to overstay my welcome, left promptly, the bell above the door clanging loudly as I stepped back into the 21st century and its market economy. I doubt the old men had any illusions about my visit, just another tragic Polish migrant trying to buy back her childhood.

LEFT Olga Boznańska's *Kwiaciarki* ("Flower Girls") in Kraków's National Gallery shows young girls preparing bouquets of flowers to sell in the Kraków market. Boznańska, with Wyspiański and others, was part of *Młoda Polska* (Young Poland), an avant-garde artistic movement in literature, painting, and theatre that started in Kraków in 1890. Many Poles know their beautiful works but these painters are less well known outside the country. It doesn't matter how fast you run through Europe's galleries, a painting like this has the power to stop you in your tracks and draw you into its stillness and tranquility.

Heading Home

As we drove out of Kraków our summer journey around Poland was nearly over, and I would be home for dinner. I realized that when I was small I always dreamed about living in big cities that never slept. But now a quiet village and a small house with a garden was my dream. And it was about to come true.

Hiding in my home town

In August Jelenia Góra feels sleepy and serene. There is only the occasional sound of slow footsteps and the echoing staccato of walking sticks on cobbled streets as the old carry home their loaves of bread. Everyone has left for the sea... Baltic, Mediterranean, Adriatic. I have the town to myself. I walk into an old bookshop and buy more volumes of Polish poetry. I carefully avoid looking at the newspapers cluttering the counter: I don't want to know the day, the month, the year. I don't want to be reminded about time running out, about the date on my return ticket, about my surgery appointment book. I want to sit under the shady arcades of the old town square and read my poetry, sip some dark tea from a tall glass, and eat freshly baked doughnuts with rose petal jam. I want those mountains on the horizon to hide me a little longer.

Doughnuts with Rose Petal Jam § PĄCZKI

My grandmother filled these yeasty buns with jam made from the rose petals I gathered, then left them to puff up under towels on tables and chairs, sofas, and sideboards. Visitors, attracted by the yeasty smell of summer baking, had to be careful where they sat.

MAKES 20 DOUGHNUTS

2 WHOLE EGGS

1 kg (2 lb 3 oz) PLAIN (ALL-PURPOSE) FLOUR

500 ml (17 fl oz) WARM FULL-CREAM MILK

110 g (4 oz) FRESH YEAST (OR 50 g (2 oz) DRY POWDERED YEAST)

4 EGG YOLKS

200 g (7 oz) CASTER SUGAR

RIND AND JUICE OF 1 LEMON

1 TABLESPOON SPIRITUS OR PURE SPIRIT

110 g (4 oz) BUTTER, MELTED

400 g (14 oz) ROSE PETAL JAM (SEE PAGE 12)

2 l (4 PINTS) VEGETABLE OIL FOR DEEP FRYING

125 g (5 oz) ICING (POWDERED) SUGAR

FOR THE GLAZE

2 TABLESPOONS ICING (POWDERED) SUGAR

1–2 TEASPOONS WATER OR FRESHLY SQUEEZED LEMON JUICE

2 DROPS ALMOND ESSENCE

Place the eggs, 120 g (4 oz) of the flour, and 250 ml (8 fl oz) of the milk with the yeast in a small bowl and work it together with your hands. This is your starter pastry that is going to grow and form the basis of your doughnut mix. Leave it under a clean tea or dish towel in a warm place for an hour to expand.

Beat the egg yolks and sugar together. Add the remaining flour and milk and your expanded starter pastry mix. Also add the lemon juice and rind, the spiritus, and the melted butter. Work it all together into a big ball of dough. Leave it for another hour to expand; it will double in size.

Take the dough, a handful at a time, and roll it out on a floured wooden board to a thickness of 1 cm (½ in). Cut out 7 cm (3 in) discs of pastry with an inverted tumbler. Put a teaspoon of rose petal jam or jelly in the middle of each disc, then pull the outside edges together, and pinch them to seal the doughnut so the jam is trapped inside. Roll the ball in your hand into an even sphere.

Place completed doughnuts on a flat surface under a clean towel and leave them to grow for another half hour or so.

Heat the oil. To test when the oil is hot enough, drop a marble-sized ball of pastry in and see if it fizzes. If so, drop a doughnut in – it should float in the oil. When the submerged underside is golden, roll it over so the top gets cooked too. Remove after a couple of minutes and allow to drain on a paper towel.

Once cool, dust the doughnuts with icing (powdered) sugar. If you prefer to glaze them, make a thin icing by mixing 2 tablespoons of icing sugar with either 1–2 teaspoons of water (with 2 drops of almond essence) or 1–2 teaspoons of freshly squeezed lemon juice.

A New Polish Home

It is now more than 60 years since my grandmother and great-grandparents were allocated half a German farmhouse in a remote mountain village in a new part of Poland. Despite their forced resettlement they fell in love with this place and a share of this house has remained in my family ever since. A few years ago the other half came up for sale. Simon was determined to buy it. Soon we were the proud owners of the house and garden where so many of my childhood memories belonged. We have cooked Józefa's recipes where she first showed me how to make *pierogi*, and we store our own preserves in the cellar. Our Australian-born children have all visited in the years since, played in the fields around the house, cutting tunnels in the long grass, throwing "Pooh sticks" in the river that runs through the garden. And a few years ago my cousin and his wife had a baby daughter, a little sister for their son. So now once again there is a little girl running round the place, getting lost among the wildflowers in the fields outside the farmhouse.

RIGHT The old German farmhouse today with both "halves" restored.

Returning to Poland and browsing through old family albums brought back so many memories. My grandfather looked so young in the photos of

him with my grandmother. What was he like? Why did he die? I remember quizzing my grandmother and watching her try to swallow her tears while attempting to answer my relentless questions. I was surprised she was still crying so long after her husband had died. It seemed 30 years was not long enough for her to forget. Like other war widows, she had to summon up all her courage to answer her children and grandchildren.

Only now I understand how strong she must have been to live a normal life without her beloved husband. Her cooking made her family happy, gave her children joy while she must have been feeling lonely, missing her husband's embraces and love. I believe now that the feel of the bread dough, the strong aromas of yeast, cloves, and rose petal jam, helped keep a 26-year-old widow rooted in the world of the living, safe from grief and despair.

I like to hope that Józefa passed her courage on to me, her granddaughter. Like her, I ended up travelling far from where I was born to live in a strange new place, which I learned to love. Thanks to her, I understand that life is an exhilarating journey, that unexpected changes and emotions need to be embraced and not feared. Our family recipes are as important as family photos: they connect distant generations like strains of DNA, and there is rose petal jam in mine.

I dedicate this book to my grandmother Józefa, my Mama Druga.

RIGHT The last photo taken of grandmother Jozefa and grandfather Rudl together, saying goodbye in Lwów, at the beginning of the Second World War. Rudi was killed in 1943. BELOW "Farewelling a Revolutionary" by Artur Grottger, 1866.

DENMARK

THE BALTIC SEA

Łeba

Sopot
Gdańsk

Malbork

Toruń

Żelazo
Wola

Łowicz

WIELKOPOLSKA

Poznań

Kórnik

GERMANY

Częstochowa

Jelenia Wrocław
Góra

Śnieżka
KARKANOSZE
MOUNTAINS

Krzeszów

LOWER
SILESIA

Kraków

C Z E C H
R E P U B L I C

Zakopane
PEAK

S L O V A K I

A U S T R I A

H U

MAP OF POLAND

RUSSIA

BELARUS

Warszawa

MAZOVIA

VISTULA RIVER

Zamość

KRESY

UKRAINE

Łancut

Lwów

CARPATHIAN MOUNTAINS

TATRA

GARY

KEY

Summer in Poland tour - The route

LISTA PRZEPISÓW

315

List of Recipes

ℐ𝓃𝒹𝑒𝓍

Numbers in *italics* refer to illustrations.

A

Angel Wings 122

apples
Apple Pancakes 174
Apple Tea 242
apple vodka 263
Roast Duck with Apples 229

Aunt Sabina's Silesian Dumplings 100

Australia 78

B

Bach, Johann Sebastian
Air on a G String 240

Bacon Spread on Rye Bread 138

Baltic Sea 178–189, 206

Batory, King Stefan 258

Bautista, Conchita 207

beef
Pierogi with Beef 65
Polish Beef Goulash 104

beetroot
Beetroot-shoot Soup 156
Sweet Pureed Beetroot 104

Bellotto, Bernardo
The Square by the Royal Castle
(*Krakowskie Przedmieście*) 223

Berlin
Prussian State Library 95

Białowieża Forest 263

biscuits
Angel Wings 122
Spiced Gingerbread Biscuits 216

Black Madonna 56

Bodo, Eugeniusz 226, *226, 232–3*
I had a date with her at nine
(*Umówiłem się z nią na dziewiątą*) 226

Bolesław the Brave 163

Boznańska, Olga 299
Flower Girls (*Kwiaciarki*) *298, 299*

bryndza cheese 272–3, *273*

Brzechwa, Jan
Pan Kleks 260, *261*

Brzeżany 39

buckwheat
Józefa's Rissoles with Mushrooms and Buckwheat 49
Pierogi with Buckwheat and Cheese 66

C

cabbage
Cabbage Rolls 284
Pasta with Mushrooms and Cabbage 50
Red Cabbage Salad 254
White Cabbage and Carrot Salad 254

cakes
Elizabeth's Honeycake with Plum Jam 221
Poppy-seed Cake 26

Carpathian mountains 266

Carpathian Vanilla Torte 270

carrots
Carrot and Sultana Salad 257
White Cabbage and Carrot Salad 254

Cauliflower Soup 98

cheese
bryndza 272–3, *273*
oscypek 272–3, *273*
Pierogi with Buckwheat and Cheese 66
Pierogi with Cheese and Potato 62

cherries
Pierogi with Sour Cherries 294
Sour Cherry Liqueur 32

chicken
Lidia's Roast Chicken 126

Chocolate Waffles 236

Chopin, Fryderyk 225, 238

Copernicus, Nicolaus 164, 210, 216, 282
De revolutionibus orbium coelestium 164, *164*

cucumbers
Cucumber Salad 152
Józefa's Cucumber Soup 154
Pickled Cucumbers 22

Częstochowa
Jasna Góra monastery 56

Czech Republic 110

Czerwone Gitary 162, *162*

Czorsztyn Castle 264, *265*

D

desserts
Carpathian Vanilla Torte 270
Misia's Strawberry Meringue 203

Acknowledgements

The authors would like to thank the following individuals and institutions for their kind permission to reproduce material in this book.

Krystyna Brzechwa
Jan Brzechwa (1090–1966): "W Szczebrzeszynie chrząszcz brzmi w trzcinie" [p.260]

Spółdzielnia Wydawnicza "Czytelnik"
J.M. Szancer (1902–1973): cover illustration for Jan Brzechwa's *Pan Kleks*, first published by Czytelnik [p.261]

Katarzyna Lengren and Yoram Gross
Zbigniew Lengren (1919–2003): "Filutek", 1973 [pp.214 and 215]

Janusz Kondratowicz
Janusz Kondratowicz (b. 1940): "*Powrócisz tu/ You will come back here*", 1965 (music written by Piotr Figiel, b. 1940) [p.208]

Libreria Editrice Vaticana
Extract from Karol Wojtyła (Pope John Paul II) (1920–2005): "Song of the Inexhaustible Sun", 1979, from *Song of the Hidden God* [p.246]

Musée du Louvre, Paris
Bernardo Bellotto, also known as Canaletto II (1720–1780): "The Square by the Royal Castle/ *Krakowskie Przedmieście*", 1768 [p.222]

National Gallery, Kraków
Olga Boznańska (1865–1940): "Flower Girls/ *Kwiaciarki*" [p.298]
Artur Grottger (1837–1867): "Farewelling a revolutionary/*Pożegnanie powstańca*", 1866 [p.310]
Tadeusz Makowski (1882–1932): "Little Gioconda – Angelina/*Mała Gioconda – Angelina*", 1920 [p.14]
Józef Pankiewicz (1866–1940): "Girl in a Red Dress/*Dziewczynka w czerwonej sukience*", 1897 [p.205]
Stanisław Wyspiański (1869–1907): "Helenka with a Mug/*Helenka z kubkiem*", 1902 [p.55]

National Gallery, Poznań
Wacław Roman Przybylski: "Portrait of Ignacy Jan Paderewski" [p.225]

National Library of Poland, Kórnik
Extract from Nicolaus Copernicus: *De revolutionibus celestium orbium* [p.164]
Medieval religious xylograph [p.164]

Czesław Miłosz Inc. and HarperCollins Publishers
Czesław Miłosz (1911–2004): "A Parable of the Poppy/ *Przypowieść o maku*", from The Separate Notebooks (A Bi-lingual Edition), © 1984, translation by Robert Hass [p.28]

Royal Castle, Warsaw
Rembrandt (1606–1669): "The Girl in a Picture Frame", also known as "The Jewish Bride", 1641, photographed by Andrzej Ring [p.225]

Wisława Szymborska
Wisława Szymborska (b. 1923): "Psalm", translation by Clare Cavanagh and Stanisław Barańczak [p.112]

Marcel Weyland
Translation of extracts from Adam Mickiewicz (1798–1855): "Pan Tadeusz", Book I: The Estate, and Book II: The Castle, 1834 [pp.239 and 250]

Walter Whipple
Translation of Cyprian Kamil Norwid (1821–1883): "My Song II/*Moja Piosenka II*", 1871 [p.79]

The authors would like to thank the following people for generous advice, practical help, and support producing this book:

Alicja Gęślak, Charles Target, Curtis Stone, Diana Henry, Edyta Głogowska, Elżbieta Kopff, Prof. Gabriela Lorenc-Plucińska, Grzegorz Zatorski and Lidia Zatorska, Henryk and Joanna Dumin, Jerzy and Norberta Smołka, Katarzyna Lengren, Lucy Carlow, Lucy Rushbrooke, Maciej and Małgorzata Bajor, Marcel Weyland, Mary Small, Matka Ksieni Edyta Wójcik OSB, Mike Zatorski, Mirosława Gil, Nick Barry, Szymon Januszkiewicz, Wojciech Wiśniewski, Yoram and Sandra Gross, and Zofia Kozłowska.

Special thanks to Jan Bajor for use of his superb black and white photographs, Lidia Zatorska and Sabina Bajor for generously supplying and testing recipes, Miranda Harvey for her inspirational book design, and Jane Aspden for so calmly and wisely guiding this project from idea to publication.

Please visit www.rosepetaljam.co.uk for recipes, tips, and feedback.

ROSE PETAL JAM

by Beata Zatorska and Simon Target
First published in 2011 by Tabula Books, London and Sydney

www.tabulabooks.com

Copyright © Beata Zatorska and Simon Target 2011

The right of Beata Zatorska and Simon Target to be identified as Authors of this Work has been asserted by them in accordance with the Copyright, Designs, and Patents Act 1998

British Cataloguing-in-Publication Data

A catalogue record for this book is available from the British Library

Photography Simon Target

Design Miranda Harvey

Editing and Production Jane Aspden
www.janeaspden.com

Map of Poland on page 312 by David Atkinson, www.handmademaps.com

ISBN 978-0-9566992-0-6

To order please contact
www.tabulabooks.com

Typeset in PP Declaration, Adobe Garamond, and Avenir

Printed and bound in China by 1010 Printing International Ltd